Making
Country
Furniture

Making Country Furniture

Alex Webb

B. T. Batsford Ltd, London

First published 1986
© Alex Webb 1986

ISBN 0 7134 4688 9

Typeset by Tek-Art Ltd, Kent
Printed in Great Britain
by Anchor Brendon Ltd,
Tiptree, Essex
for the Publishers,
B T Batsford Ltd,
4 Fitzhardinge Street,
London W1H 0AH

Contents

Acknowledgement

I would like to thank Diane for the typing, mainly from my illegible notes; Photocentre, Eastbourne, for taking the photographs; and the administrators of Michelham Priory, Upper Dicker, near Hailsham, East Sussex, for allowing me the use of the grounds to shoot the pictures.

Note:

While every effort has been made to ensure that the measurements given in this book are correct, readers are advised to guard against possible error by making frequent checks of all measurements as work on the construction of each piece progresses. Use either metric or imperial all the way through a piece; don't mix them.

Introduction

Furniture made by the village or country carpenter for the farms and smaller homes scattered throughout the countryside during the seventeenth, eighteenth and nineteenth centuries had to fulfil two basic requirements: it had to be functional, and it had to be built to last a lifetime. The choice of timber for making a piece of furniture was usually left to the carpenter's own expertise as, in many cases, was the design. The design for a piece of furniture would be based on strength and simplicity. Consider, for example, a dresser. The location in the house would be measured to give the carpenter the overall dimensions, and the items of china, cutlery, crocks and pans which it would have to take would be given. With these details he would build a piece of furniture using a method of construction that had been well tried and tested over many years; a piece of furniture that would accommodate the utensils for which it was specifically made, and would probably continue to do so for many generations.

This book describes eight pieces of country-style furniture, giving a step-by-step guide to their construction. The designs, like all country furniture, are kept simple, and the method of construction used has been established over many hundreds of years. The result will be furniture that is strong, sturdy and functional, with the warmth and charm that only country-style furniture gives.

Most wood yards hold a good selection of well-seasoned boards suitable for furniture making; oak, ash, elm, sycamore, beech and pine are perhaps the most common, although timbers such as yew, apple and cherry can also be found. In fact, if a tree is large enough to plank, the chances are it will be found in a wood yard somewhere. Perhaps the best method of locating the timber of your choice is to look in the telephone directory; wood yards are surprisingly numerous, and if they do not have what you are looking for, the staff are usually quite helpful in pointing you towards another source of supply.

The finishing of a piece of furniture will depend largely on the treatment it is likely to get, and the individual's own taste. Beeswax or linseed oil is probably the best form of treatment for solid wood, and both are relatively easy to apply. However, they do need to be maintained. There are many varnishes, polishes, stains and waxes on the market today which are easy to apply, and are in some ways more suitable for present-day needs.

A point which must be remembered when buying timber is that sizes vary considerably. For example, sawn timber sold as 50mm (2in) can sometimes measure as much as 57mm (2¼in), whereas prepared timber (planed) sold as 50mm (2in) can measure 45mm (1¾in).

Although the measurements in this book are exact, it may in some cases be advisable to alter slightly the size of the piece of furniture to suit the wood sizes available or the purpose of the piece of furniture, so check your measurements carefully at all stages; mistakes can be time-consuming and expensive.

Tools

The furniture in this book has all been made using on purpose only the tools that the average enthusiast would have, or be able to obtain easily, without a great deal of expense.

Hardware shops and large stores usually hold a good selection of tools, and since the tools required are just the basic ones, no trouble should be found in obtaining them.

❑ Panelled Chest

Panelled chests of this type were first seen during the sixteenth century and nearly always made from oak. Their main purpose was to house and protect such items as clothes, blankets and linens from the damp and musty conditions which existed in many of the homes at that time.

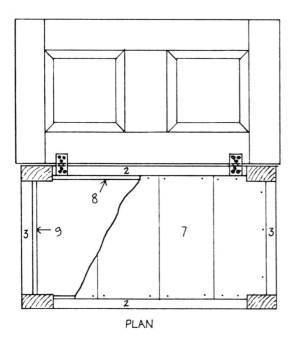

PLAN

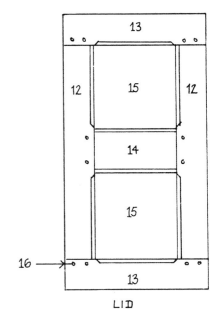

LID

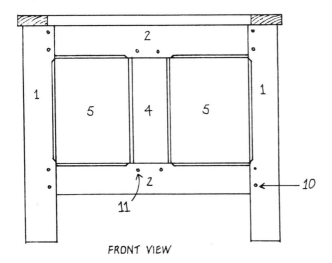

FRONT VIEW

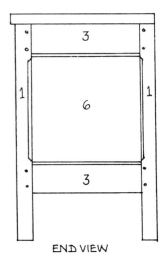

END VIEW

MATERIALS

Part no.	Part name	No. of pieces	Size	
1	Legs	4	686 × 99 × 48mm	(27 × 3⅞ × 1⅞in)
2	Rails, top and bottom, front and back	4	736 × 99 × 32mm	(29 × 3⅞ × 1¼in)
3	End rails, top and bottom	4	413 × 99 × 32mm	(16¼ × 3⅞ × 1¼in)
4	Centre upright rails, front and back	2	381 × 140 × 32mm	(15 × 5½ × 1¼in)
5	Panels, front and back	4	343 × 260 × 13mm	(13½ × 10¼ × ½in)
6	End panels	2	375 × 343 × 13mm	(14¾ × 13½ × ½in)
7	Coffer bottom	*	775 × 394 × 13mm	(30½ × 15½ × ½in)
8	Bottom support battens	2	635 × 19 × 19mm	(25 × ¾ × ¾in)
9	Bottom support battens	2	362 × 19 × 19mm	(14¼ × ¾ × ¾in)
10	Dowel pegs	32	38 × 6.4mm	(1½ × ¼in)
11	Dowel pegs	8	25 × 6.4mm	(1 × ¼in)

Chest lid

Part no.	Part name	No. of pieces	Size	
12	Rails, front and back	2	775 × 99 × 32mm	(30½ × 3⅞ × 1¼in)
13	End rails	2	470 × 99 × 32mm	(18½ × 3⅞ × 1¼in)
14	Centre rail	1	375 × 140 × 32mm	(14¾ × 5½ × 1¼in)
15	Panels	2	286 × 279 × 13mm	(11¼ × 11 × ½in)
16	Dowel pegs	12	25 × 6.4mm	(1 × ¼in)

Wood glue
1 pair of back flap hinges, 44 × 67mm (1¾ × 2⅝in), and screws to fix
16 panel pins, 38mm (1½in)
22 panel pins, 25mm (1in)

* number depends on board widths available

Panelled chest showing part numbers.
Top size: 470 × 876mm (18½ × 34½in)
Height: 718mm (28¼in)
Timber: pine
Finish: clear varnish

Fig. 1

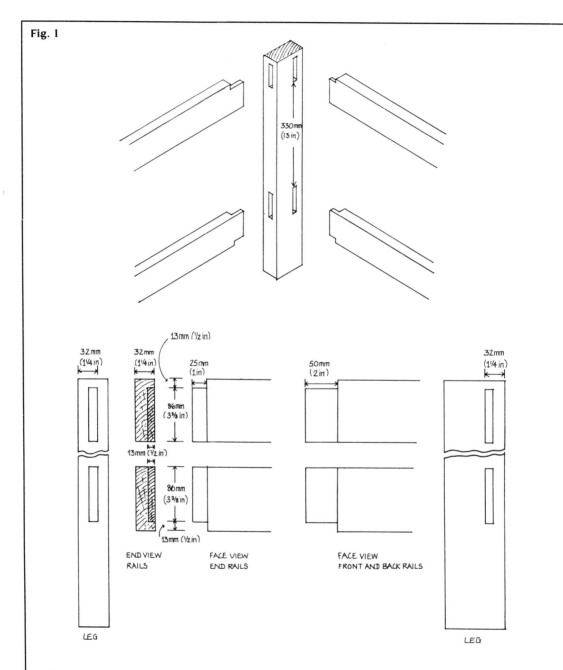

330mm
(13 in)

32mm
(1¼ in)

32mm
(1¼ in)

13mm (½ in)

25mm
(1 in)

86mm
(3⅜ in)

13mm (½ in)

86mm
(3⅜ in)

13mm (½ in)

50mm
(2 in)

32mm
(1¼ in)

END VIEW
RAILS

FACE VIEW
END RAILS

FACE VIEW
FRONT AND BACK RAILS

LEG

LEG

The joints

Mark and cut all mortise and tenon joints for the legs and rails to the sizes shown in fig. 1 (see also 'Mortise and Tenon Joints, *page* 134), trying each one to make sure a satisfactory fit has been obtained.

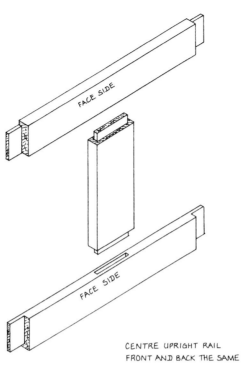

FACE SIDE

FACE SIDE

CENTRE UPRIGHT RAIL
FRONT AND BACK THE SAME

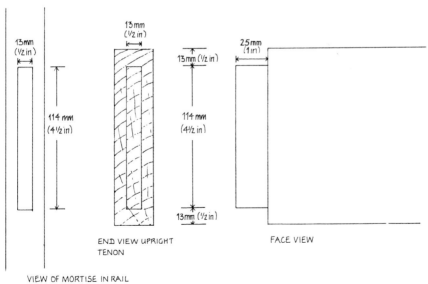

13 mm
(½ in)

114 mm
(4½ in)

VIEW OF MORTISE IN RAIL

13 mm
(½ in)

13 mm (½ in)

114 mm
(4½ in)

13 mm (½ in)

END VIEW UPRIGHT
TENON

25 mm
(1 in)

FACE VIEW

Fig. 2

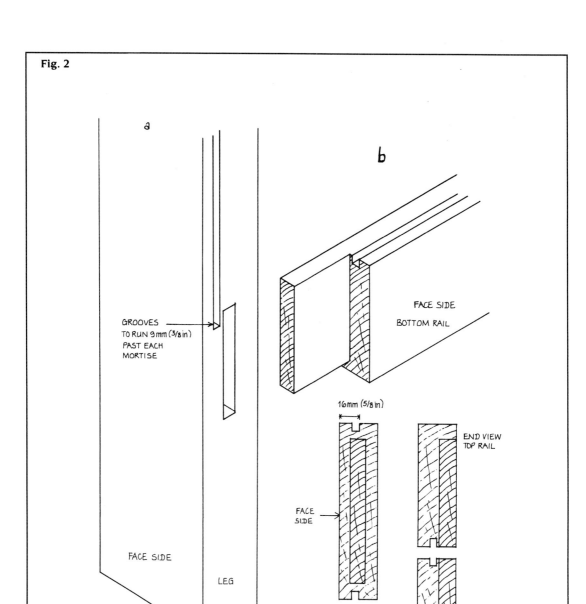

a

GROOVES
TO RUN 9mm (3/8 in)
PAST EACH
MORTISE

FACE SIDE

LEG

b

FACE SIDE

BOTTOM RAIL

16mm (5/8 in)

FACE
SIDE

END VIEW
TOP RAIL

END VIEW
CENTRE UPRIGHT

END VIEW
BOTTOM RAIL

Grooves to house panels

The grooves that house the panels in the framework are normally made using a router or a rebate plane. If neither of these tools is available a chisel can be used, following the same instructions as for cutting out a mortise.

Working from the face side on all pieces, make a groove 6.4 × 6.4 × 16mm (1/4 × 1/4 × 5/8in) from the edge (fig. 2). The groove cut in the rails runs the full length, whereas the groove in the legs stops about 9mm (3/8in) past the mortise (fig. 2a).

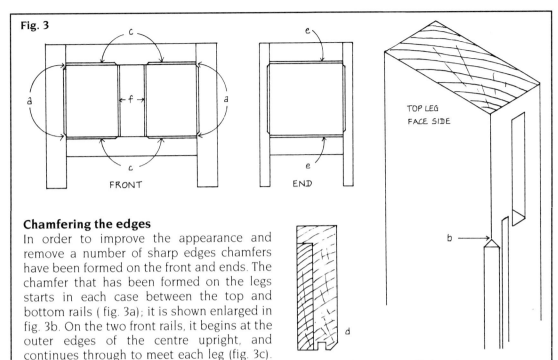

Fig. 3

FRONT

END

TOP LEG
FACE SIDE

Chamfering the edges

In order to improve the appearance and remove a number of sharp edges chamfers have been formed on the front and ends. The chamfer that has been formed on the legs starts in each case between the top and bottom rails (fig. 3a); it is shown enlarged in fig. 3b. On the two front rails, it begins at the outer edges of the centre upright, and continues through to meet each leg (fig. 3c). Also shown is the end view of the rail (fig. 3d). On the end rails (fig. 3e) it continues the whole length of the rail, as it does on the centre upright (fig. 3f). All chamfers are 6.4mm (¼in) in depth, and have an end angle of 45°. (See also Mouldings, *page* 127).

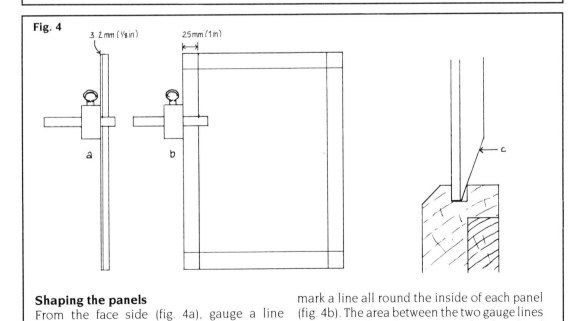

Fig. 4

3.2 mm (⅛ in)

25mm (1 in)

Shaping the panels

From the face side (fig. 4a), gauge a line 3.2mm (⅛in) in around all four edges of each panel. Reset the gauge to 25mm (1in) and mark a line all round the inside of each panel (fig. 4b). The area between the two gauge lines can now be planed away, giving the chamfered inner edge (fig. 4c).

At this point a trial assembly is advisable, mainly to ensure that there are no minor faults or obstructions which are likely to prevent the joints or the panels from going together fully. Once this has been done, assembly can begin.

Fig. 5

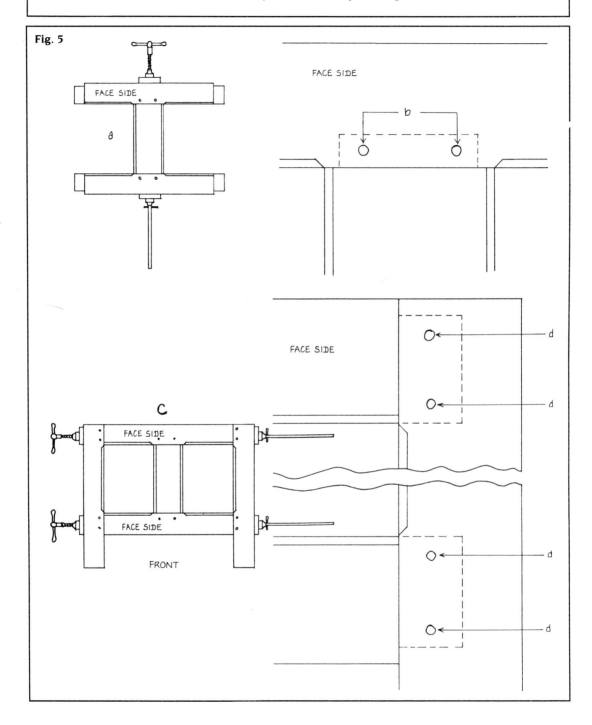

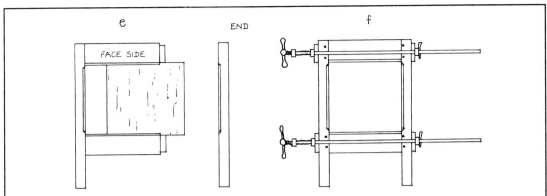

e   FACE SIDE   END   f

Assembly

Run glue into the mortises of the top and bottom rails, front. Push the rails onto the centre upright and cramp up (fig. 5a). With a 6.4mm (¼in) bit, drill two holes in each joint a depth of about 29mm (1⅛in) in the positions shown in fig. 5b. Squeeze a blob of glue into each hole and tap home the down pegs. Remove the cramp, wipe away any surplus glue, then put the frame to one side. Repeat the same procedure with the back. Next, squeeze glue into the mortise on the two front legs. Slide the two front panels into place. Push the legs onto the front frame and cramp up (fig. 5c). Drill two 6.4mm (¼in) holes in each tenon in the position shown in fig. 5d, to a depth of about 38mm (1½in). Glue and peg as before. Repeat the same procedure with the back. Finally, squeeze glue into the four mortises on the inside of the front legs. Push home the four end rails (fig. 5e), and slide in the panel. Squeeze glue into the remaining four mortises located in the back legs, push the back onto the tenons and cramp up (fig. 5f).

Fig. 6

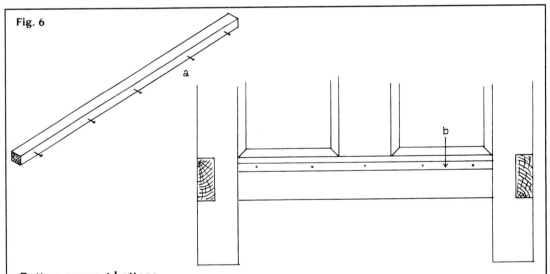

a   b

Bottom support battens

The battens which support the chest bottom can now be fixed into place. Tap five 38mm (1½in) panel pins into each of the two long battens so that the pin tips just show through the batten (fig. 6a). Smear glue along the whole length of the batten and nail into position 13mm (½in) below the top of the bottom rail (fig. 6b). The end support battens each have three 38mm (1½in) panel pins and should be glued and fixed in the same way.

Fig. 7

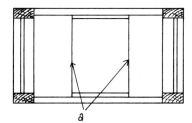

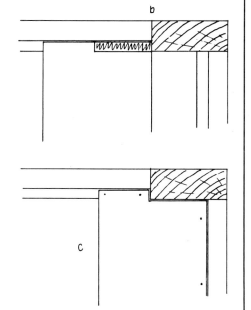

b

c

Chest bottom

The chest bottom is made up from several boards butted together but not glued, which makes it relatively easy to fix. Lower two of the boards into the chest bottom and push each one as far as it will go towards the opposite ends (fig. 7a). You will see that in each corner part of the leg restricts the boards from reaching the end rail, and a section must be removed from each bottom corner. This is done by measuring the distance by which the board is short of the end rail and squaring a line onto the board from either the front or back rail, depending on which corner is being marked. The second line is obtained by drawing a line on the board parallel to the inside edge of the leg to reach the first line (fig. 7b). When all corners have been marked, take out the boards, cut away the corner pieces and drop back into the correct position (fig. 7c). The remaining boards simply drop in until the bottom is complete. They are then pinned into position using the 25mm (1in) panel pins. This completes the construction of the base.

Lid

Fig. 8

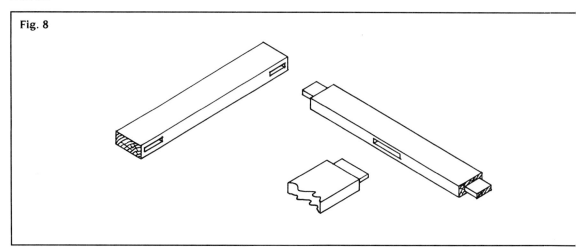

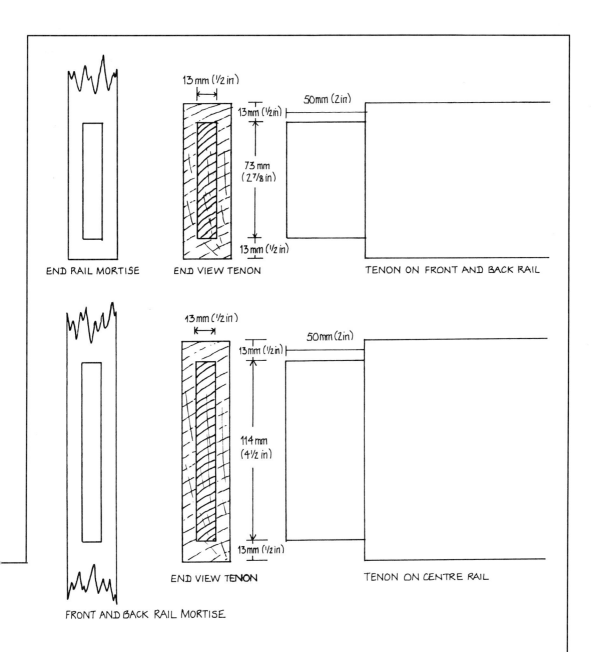

13 mm (½ in)

13 mm (½ in)

50mm (2in)

73 mm (2⅞ in)

13 mm (½ in)

END RAIL MORTISE

END VIEW TENON

TENON ON FRONT AND BACK RAIL

13 mm (½ in)

13 mm (½ in)

50mm (2in)

114 mm (4½ in)

13mm (½in)

END VIEW TENON

TENON ON CENTRE RAIL

FRONT AND BACK RAIL MORTISE

Joints

The principle of constructing the chest lid is the same as for making the base, the differences being only in the size of the joints. Mark and cut out all mortise and tenon joints to the sizes shown in fig. 8.

17

Fig. 9

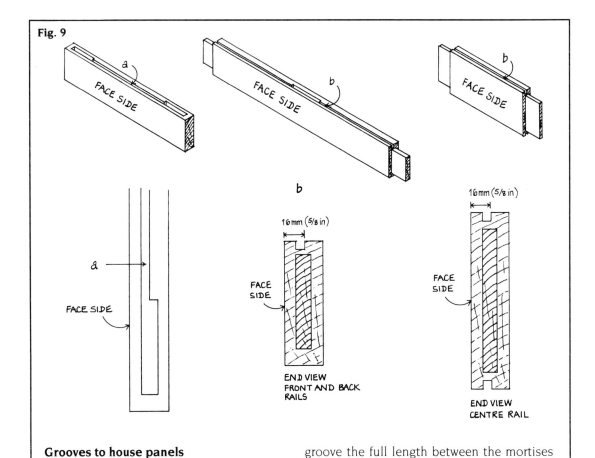

16mm (⁵⁄₈ in)

16mm (⁵⁄₈ in)

FACE SIDE

FACE SIDE

FACE SIDE

FACE SIDE

FACE SIDE

a

b

b

a

b

FACE
SIDE

END VIEW
FRONT AND BACK
RAILS

FACE
SIDE

END VIEW
CENTRE RAIL

Grooves to house panels
Working from the face side, form a groove 6.4 × 6.4mm (¹⁄₄ × ¹⁄₄in), 16mm (⁵⁄₈in) in on all inner edges (fig. 9). On both end rails run the groove the full length between the mortises (fig. 9a). On the front and back rails and on the centre rail, all grooves run the full length (fig. 9b).

Chamfering the edges
The chamfering on the lid is an exact copy of that on the chest front, and the instructions in fig. 3 can be followed.

Shaping the panels
The two panels can now be shaped by following the instructions in fig. 4.

Assembly
It is now advisable to do a trial assembly, checking carefully that joints and panels come together satisfactorily. If all is well the lid can be glued, clamped and pegged by following the instructions for gluing up the front (fig. 5a, b, c and d). The lid has now been completed.

Fig. 10

Fixing the hinges

To fit the hinges, first support the chest lid in exactly the position it will be when open (fig. 10a). Lay the hinges in position as shown in fig. 10b, 127mm (5in) in from the end of the lid, the knuckle of the hinge being the gap between the lid and the back rail (fig. 10c), and mark all round with a pencil. Mark also the thickness of the hinge flap on the appropriate edges.

Fig. 10

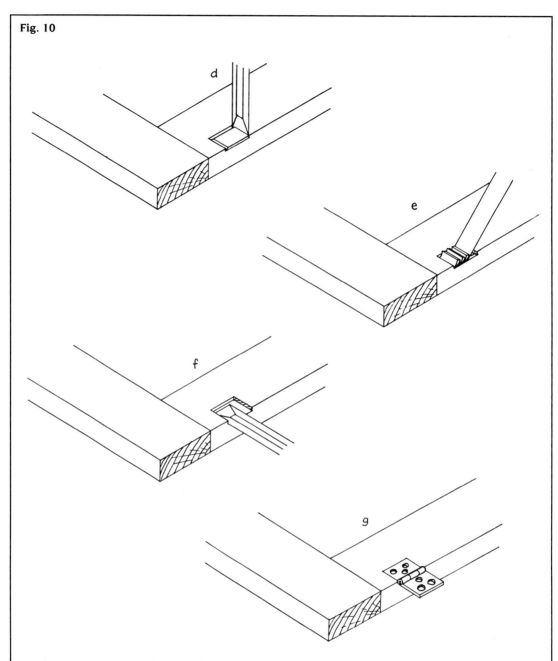

Keeping carefully to the pencil line, tap a chisel into the wood to the depth of the hinge flap (fig. 10d), to create the recessed area into which the hinge flap is to fit. Make several cuts, each about 3.2mm (⅛in) apart, tapped in to the depth of the hinge flap (fig. 10e). The loose wood can now be pared away (fig. 10f)

and the hinge flap screwed into position (fig. 10g). Having fitted both hinges, you have to remove them both again for the final jobs of sanding and applying the finish of your choice. When this has been done, the hinges can be replaced to complete the chest.

2 Cricket Table

Although it is uncertain how this table came by its name, there can be no doubt of its usefulness. This design has proved its worth over many hundreds of years, being strong, stable and versatile.

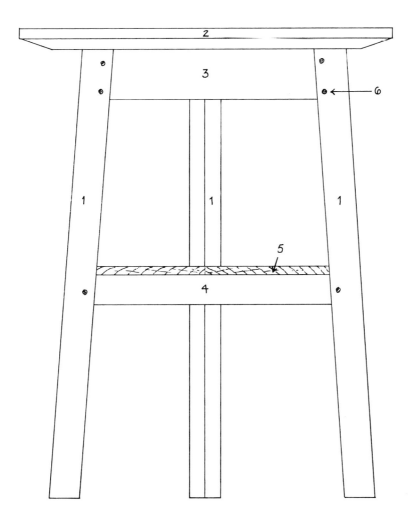

Cricket table showing part numbers.
Top size: 609mm (24in)
Height: 743mm (29¼in)
Timber: elm
Finish: stain and varnish

MATERIALS

Part no.	Part name	No. of pieces	Size	
1	Legs	3	711 × 50 × 50mm	(28 × 2 × 2in)
2	Top	*	609 × 609 × 32mm	(24 × 24 × 1¼in)
3	Top rails	3	394 × 76 × 22mm	(15½ × 3 × ⅞in)
4	Bottom rails	3	444 × 45 × 22mm	(17½ × 1¾ × ⅞in)
5	Under shelf	1	609 × 203 × 13mm	(24 × 8 × ½in)
6	Dowel pegs	18	32 × 6.4mm	(1¼ × ¼in)

Wood glue

3 no. 10 steel countersunk screws, 38mm (1½in)

11 nails, 38mm (1½in)

* number depends on board widths available

CONSTRUCTION

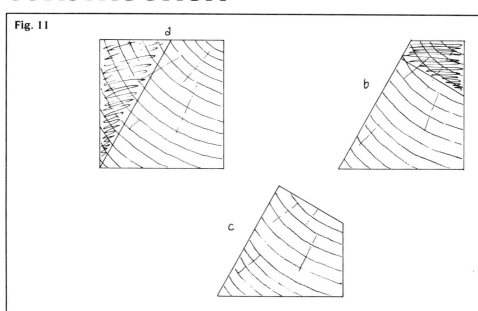

Fig. 11

Shaping the legs

On both ends of each leg draw a line at an angle of 60° as shown in fig. 11a. The area shaded in on the drawing must now be planed away. Working next from the side just planed, square a 90° line across both ends of each leg at a point 50mm (2in) up from what will become the outer edge of the leg (fig. 11b), and once again plane away the area shaded on the drawing. The shape which remains (fig. 11c) is the completed shape of the table leg.

Fig. 12

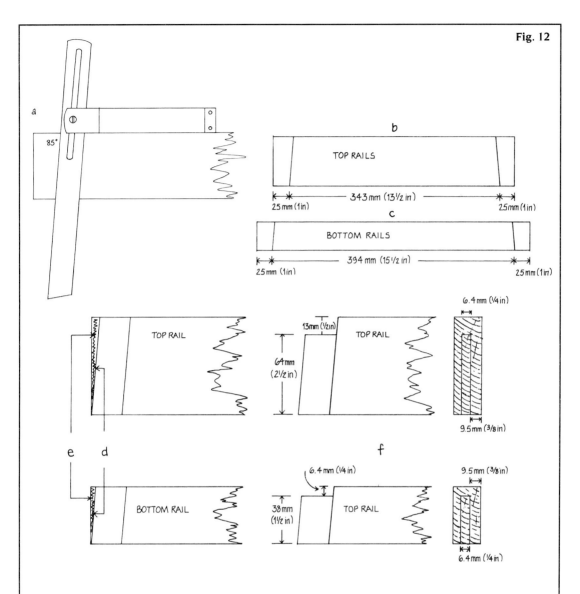

a

85°

b

TOP RAILS

25mm (1in) ←—— 343 mm (13½ in) ——→ 25mm (1in)

c

BOTTOM RAILS

25mm (1in) ←—— 394 mm (15½ in) ——→ 25mm (1in)

6.4 mm (¼ in)

TOP RAIL

TOP RAIL

13mm (½in)

64mm (2½ in)

9.5 mm (³/₈ in)

e   d

f

6.4 mm (¼ in)

9.5 mm (³/₈ in)

BOTTOM RAIL

38mm (1½ in)

TOP RAIL

6.4 mm (¼ in)

Marking and cutting the tenons

To form the splay-leg effect of this table it is necessary to angle the shoulders of the tenons. To do this, set a bevel at the angle shown in fig. 12a. This setting should be retained throughout as it is the same on all joints for both top and bottom rails. Working with the top rails first, mark a line with the bevel in the positions shown in fig. 12b, both on the face side and the inside of the rail. A square can now be used to join the lines on both top and bottom edges, thus forming a continuous line around the rail. The same procedure can now be applied to the three bottom rails using the measurements shown in fig. 12c. A further line should now be drawn with the bevel parallel to the first on all top and bottom rails at the positions shown in fig. 12d. The wedge-shaped piece left at the end of each rail (fig. 12e), should now be cut away. The remainder of the tenon can be marked and cut by following the measurement in fig. 12f. (See also Mortise and Tenon Joints, *page* 134.)

Fig. 13

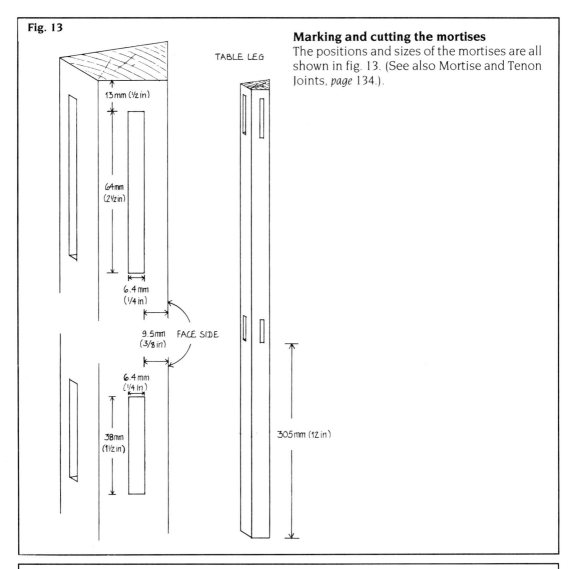

TABLE LEG

13 mm (½ in)

64mm (2½ in)

6.4 mm (¼ in)

9.5mm (3/8 in)   FACE SIDE

6.4 mm (¼ in)

38mm (1½ in)

305 mm (12 in)

Marking and cutting the mortises

The positions and sizes of the mortises are all shown in fig. 13. (See also Mortise and Tenon Joints, *page* 134.).

Fig. 14

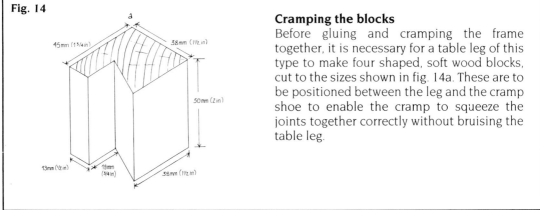

a

45mm (1¾ in)

38mm (1½ in)

50mm (2 in)

13mm (½ in)

19mm (3/4 in)

38mm (1½ in)

Cramping the blocks

Before gluing and cramping the frame together, it is necessary for a table leg of this type to make four shaped, soft wood blocks, cut to the sizes shown in fig. 14a. These are to be positioned between the leg and the cramp shoe to enable the cramp to squeeze the joints together correctly without bruising the table leg.

Fig. 14

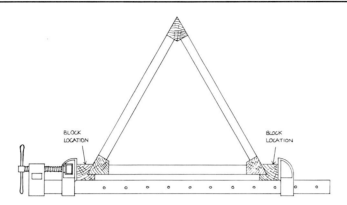

Assembly

When the cramping blocks have been made and a trial assembly has taken place to ensure that there are no minor obstructions restricting the joints from fitting, assembly can begin.

Squeeze a generous amount of glue into all joints on the three legs and push the whole table frame together. Using two sash cramps, cramp up one side at a time (fig. 14b and c). Without moving the cramps, drill two 6.4mm (¼in) holes in the joints of the top rail and one 6.4mm (¼in) hole in each bottom joint at the positions shown in fig. 14d. Squeeze a blob of glue into each hole and tap home a dowel peg in each. Any dowel peg still protruding from the leg can be cut away with a sharp chisel and surplus glue can be wiped away with a damp cloth. Remove the cramps and repeat the process with the other sides. When this has been completed, place the frame to one side for about 24 hours to allow the glue to harden off.

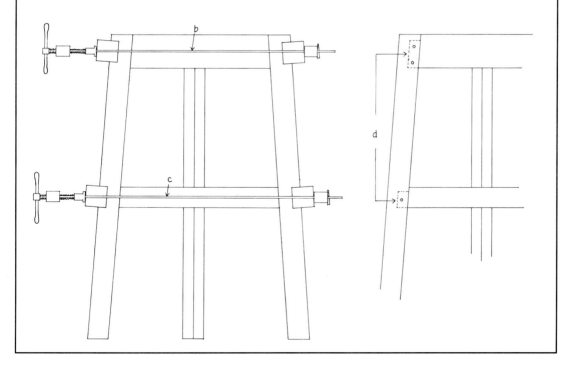

Fig. 15

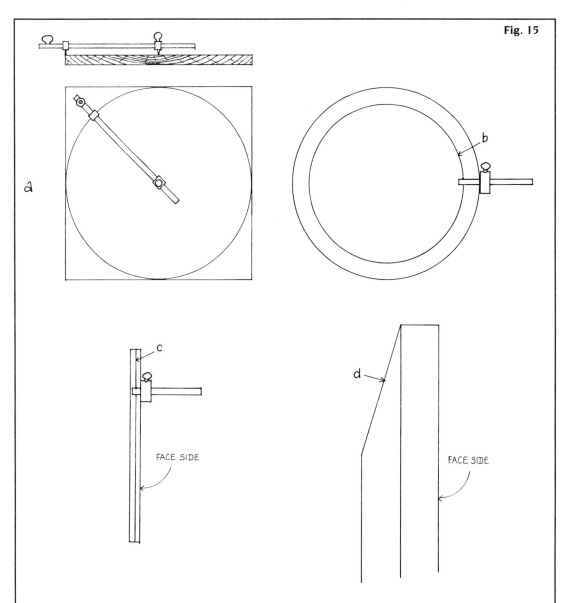

Table top

If a single plank 610mm (24in) wide cannot be obtained it will be necessary to join two or three boards to obtain the required size (see Jointing Boards Edge to Edge, *page* 136). Once the size has been obtained, mark out a circle 610mm (24in) in diameter (fig. 15a) and cut out. The edge should be planed and sanded to remove any roughness left by the saw before proceeding to the next stage. With a gauge set at 51mm (2in), mark a line on the under side of the table top (fig. 15b). Reset the gauge to 16mm (⅝in) and, working from the face side, mark a line all the way around the table top edge (fig. 15c). The area between the two gauge lines can now be planed away, giving a chamfer to the under side of the top (fig. 15d). When the table is assembled you will see that the chamfer greatly reduces the heavy look which a top of this thickness would normally have, without interfering with its strength.

Fig. 16

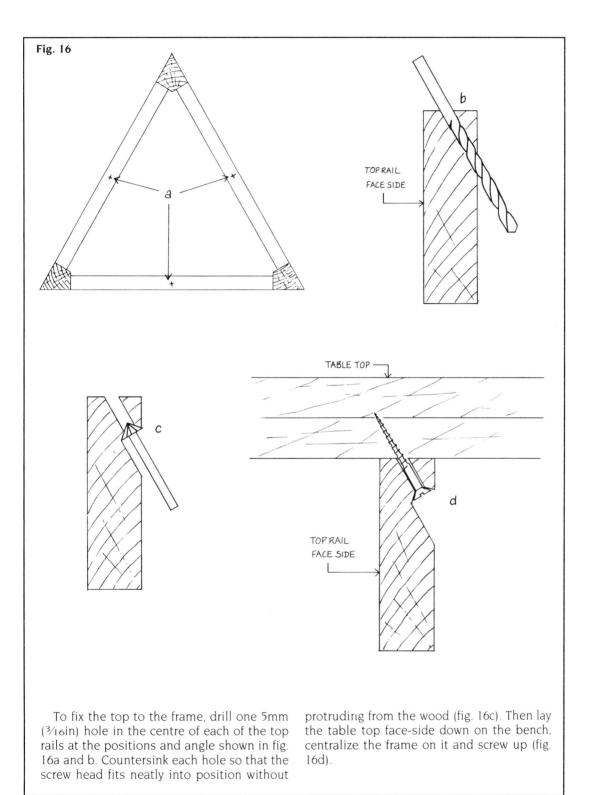

TOP RAIL
FACE SIDE

b

a

TABLE TOP

c

d

TOP RAIL
FACE SIDE

To fix the top to the frame, drill one 5mm (³⁄₁₆in) hole in the centre of each of the top rails at the positions and angle shown in fig. 16a and b. Countersink each hole so that the screw head fits neatly into position without protruding from the wood (fig. 16c). Then lay the table top face-side down on the bench, centralize the frame on it and screw up (fig. 16d).

Fig. 16

e

f

Under shelf

To complete the table assembly, mark out the under shelf as shown in fig. 16e. Cut out and lay the shelf into position over the bottom rails. The nail holes can now be marked (fig. 16f) and drilled out using a bit with a diameter the same size as that of the nail being used.

Place the nails into the holes and tap home. Then, using a nail punch, tap the heads just below the surface of the wood ready for filling.

Sand the table to a fine finish, fill any holes and apply the wax or polish of your choice.

3 Side Table

The versatility of this side table with its single drawer makes this piece of furniture as popular today as it was when first designed during the eighteenth century.

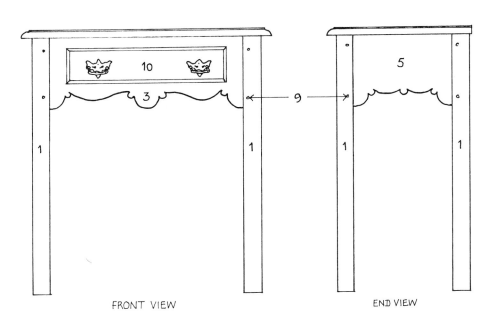

FRONT VIEW

END VIEW

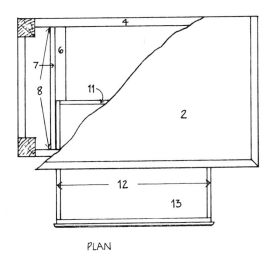

PLAN

Side table showing part numbers.
Top size: 736 × 432mm (29 × 17in)
Height: 759mm (29⅞in)
Timber: oak
Finish: oak stain and varnish

MATERIALS

Part no.	Part name	No. of pieces	Size	
1	Legs	4	736 × 50 × 50mm	(29 × 2 × 2in)
2	Top	*	736 × 432 × 22mm	(29 × 17 × 7/8in)
3	Front	1	622 × 203 × 22mm	(24 1/2 × 8 × 7/8in)
4	Back	1	622 × 203 × 22mm	(24 1/2 × 8 × 7/8in)
5	Ends	2	343 × 203 × 22mm	(13 1/2 × 8 × 7/8in)
6	Drawer runners	2	349 × 45 × 13mm	(13 3/4 × 1 3/4 × 1/2in)
7	Drawer guides	2	349 × 32 × 13mm	(13 3/4 × 1 1/4 × 1/2in)
8	Drawer runner support blocks	4	45 × 25 × 13mm	(1 3/4 × 1 × 1/2in)
9	Dowel pegs	16	32 × 6.4mm	(1 1/4 × 1/4in)

Drawer pieces

Part no.	Part name	No. of pieces	Size	
10	Front	1	470 × 102 × 22mm	(18 1/2 × 4 × 7/8in)
11	Back	1	454 × 70 × 13mm	(17 7/8 × 2 3/4 × 1/2in)
12	Sides	2	355 × 86 × 13mm	(14 × 3 3/8 × 1/2in)
13	Bottom	*	442 × 355 × 13mm	(17 3/8 × 14 × 1/2in)
	Knobs (if required)	2	76 × 38 × 38mm	(3 × 1 1/2 × 1 1/2in)

Wood glue
19 panel pins, 25mm (1in)
6 panel pins, 32mm (1 1/4in)
8 no. 8 steel countersunk screws, 38mm (1 1/2in)

* number depends on board widths available

CONSTRUCTION

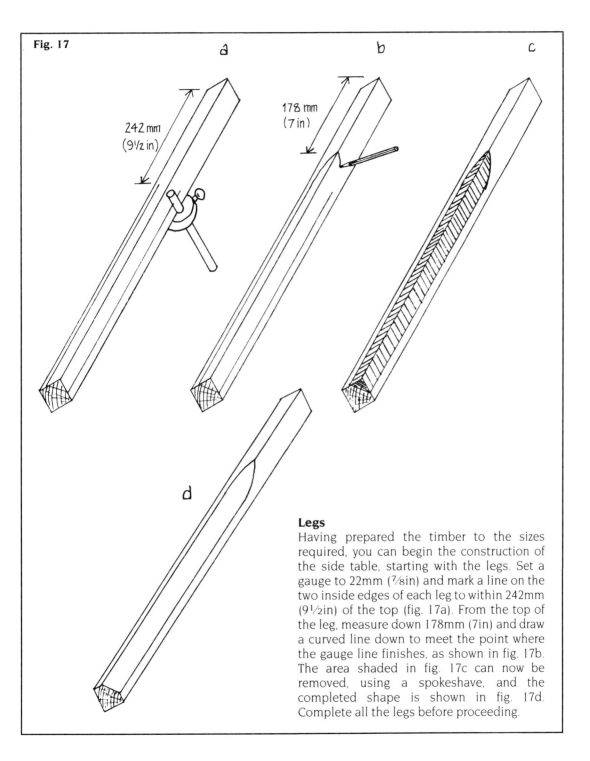

Fig. 17

a

b

c

242 mm
(9½ in)

178 mm
(7 in)

d

Legs
Having prepared the timber to the sizes
required, you can begin the construction of
the side table, starting with the legs. Set a
gauge to 22mm (⅞in) and mark a line on the
two inside edges of each leg to within 242mm
(9½in) of the top (fig. 17a). From the top of
the leg, measure down 178mm (7in) and draw
a curved line down to meet the point where
the gauge line finishes, as shown in fig. 17b.
The area shaded in fig. 17c can now be
removed, using a spokeshave, and the
completed shape is shown in fig. 17d.
Complete all the legs before proceeding.

Fig. 18

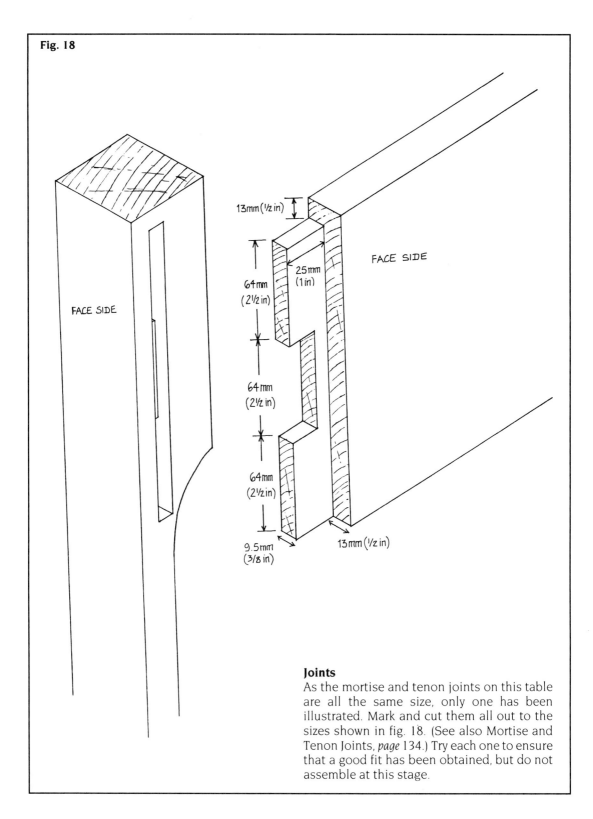

FACE SIDE

13mm (½ in)

64mm
(2½ in)

25mm
(1 in)

FACE SIDE

64mm
(2½ in)

64mm
(2½ in)

9.5mm
(3/8 in)

13mm (½ in)

Joints

As the mortise and tenon joints on this table are all the same size, only one has been illustrated. Mark and cut them all out to the sizes shown in fig. 18. (See also Mortise and Tenon Joints, *page* 134.) Try each one to ensure that a good fit has been obtained, but do not assemble at this stage.

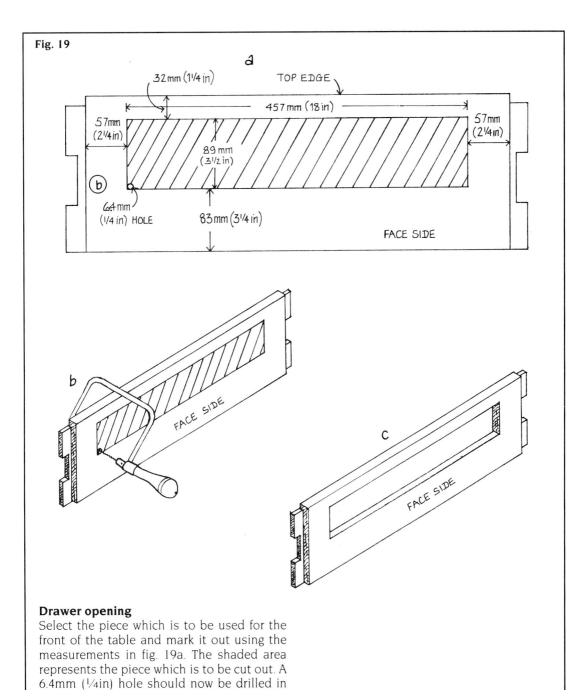

Fig. 19

32mm (1¼ in)

TOP EDGE

457mm (18 in)

57mm (2¼in)

57mm (2¼in)

89 mm (3½ in)

b

6.4mm (¼ in) HOLE

83mm (3¼ in)

FACE SIDE

b

FACE SIDE

c

FACE SIDE

Drawer opening

Select the piece which is to be used for the front of the table and mark it out using the measurements in fig. 19a. The shaded area represents the piece which is to be cut out. A 6.4mm (¼in) hole should now be drilled in the bottom left-hand corner to enable a coping saw to be inserted and the waste wood cut out (fig. 19b). Finally, sand the inside of the drawer opening to remove any roughness left after sawing. The finished opening is shown in fig. 19c.

Fig. 20

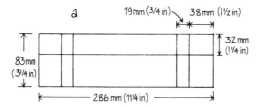

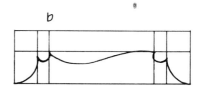

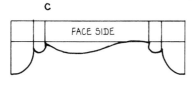

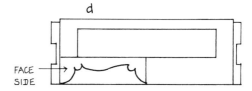

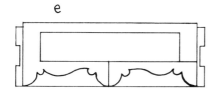

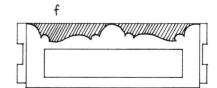

Shaping the frame

To form the shaping below the drawer front opening it is first necessary to make a cardboard template. Select, if possible, a piece of white card which is fairly stiff, and cut it to the size shown in fig. 20a. Mark on it the measurements also shown in fig. 20a. The curves which form the shaping in fig. 20b can be drawn in free-hand, or they can be marked in by using everyday items found in the home such as coins, food tins, plates etc. Having marked out the pattern, carefully cut it out with a sharp knife or a pair of scissors, keeping the piece shown in fig. 20c. At this point it is a good idea to write 'face side' on the pattern so that you avoid using it the wrong way round. Lay the pattern face-side up on the front (fig. 20d), and mark around it with a pencil. Now place the pattern face-side down on the right-hand side of the front (fig. 20e), and again mark around it with a pencil. Keep the pattern as it will be used again to mark the table sides. Turn the front upside down and secure in a vice. The shaded area shown in fig. 20f can now be cut away with a coping saw and any roughness remaining can be removed by sandpapering.

Fig. 21

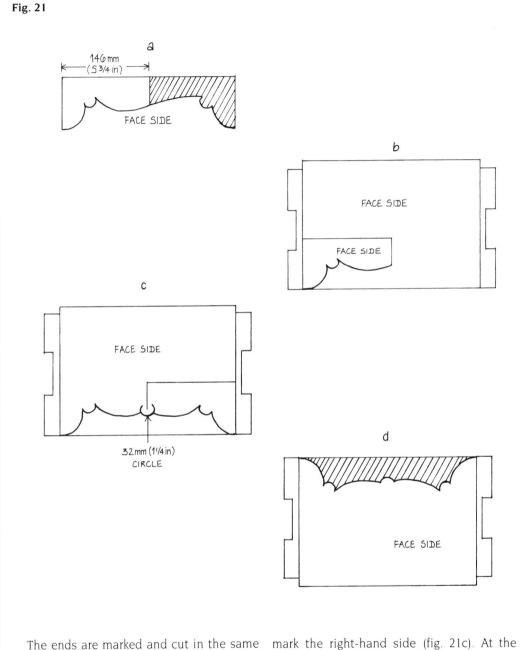

a

146 mm
(5 3/4 in)

FACE SIDE

b

FACE SIDE

FACE SIDE

c

FACE SIDE

32 mm (1 1/4 in)
CIRCLE

d

FACE SIDE

The ends are marked and cut in the same way as the front, but the template used on the front now needs to be shortened. Measure from the left-hand side 146mm (5¾in) as shown in fig. 21a and cut, keeping the left-hand piece. Use this to mark the left-hand side first (fig. 21b), and then face-side down to mark the right-hand side (fig. 21c). At the point in the centre where the two meet, draw a circle about 32mm (1¼in) in diameter (fig. 21c). Secure upside down in a vice and with a coping saw remove the area shaded in fig. 21d. Again remove any roughness by sanding.

Fig. 22

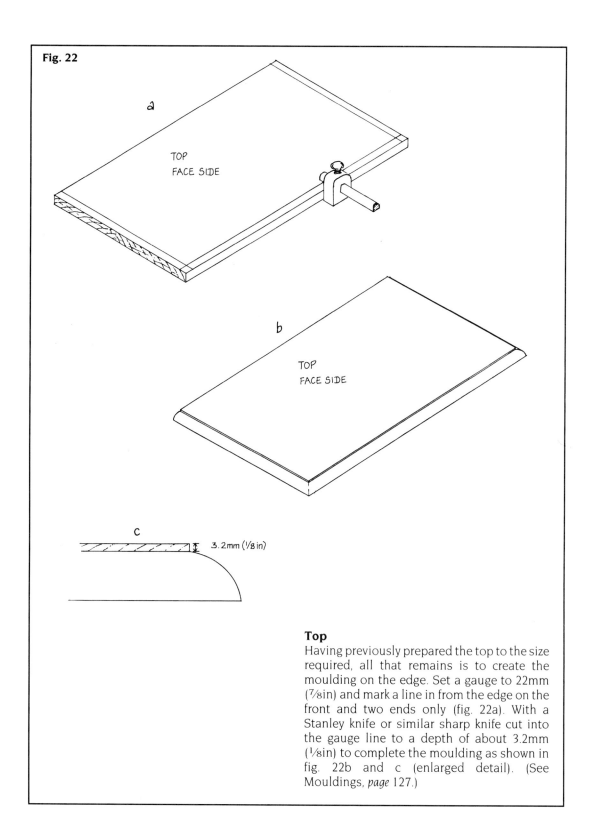

a

TOP
FACE SIDE

b

TOP
FACE SIDE

c

3.2mm (⅛in)

Top
Having previously prepared the top to the size required, all that remains is to create the moulding on the edge. Set a gauge to 22mm (⅞in) and mark a line in from the edge on the front and two ends only (fig. 22a). With a Stanley knife or similar sharp knife cut into the gauge line to a depth of about 3.2mm (⅛in) to complete the moulding as shown in fig. 22b and c (enlarged detail). (See Mouldings, *page* 127.)

Fig. 23

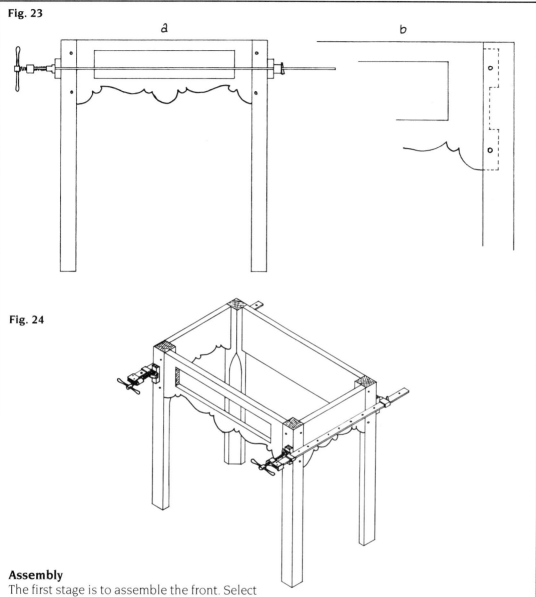

Fig. 24

Assembly

The first stage is to assemble the front. Select the two legs which are to be used for the front of the table and squeeze a good coating of glue into the mortises. Push the legs onto the tenons and cramp up (fig. 23a), remembering to use wooden blocks between the legs and the cramp shoes. Next, drill two 6.4mm (¼in) holes in each joint to a depth of at least 32mm (1¼in), roughly through the centre of each tenon (fig. 23b). Squeeze a blob of glue into each hole and with a mallet tap the dowel pegs in to finish flush with the surface. Remove the cramp and repeat the same process with the back. When both front and back have been completed, squeeze glue into the remaining mortises, push on the ends, then cramp and peg together as described for fixing the front (figs. 23 and 24). The assembled frame should now be placed to one side for about 24 hours to allow the glue to harden.

Drawer Supports

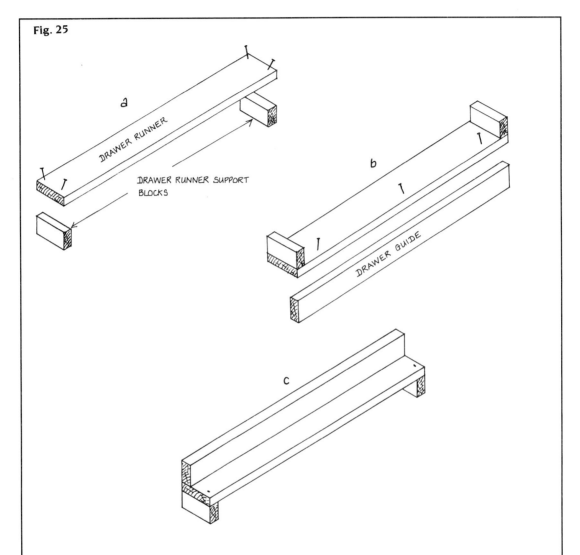

Fig. 25

a

DRAWER RUNNER

DRAWER RUNNER SUPPORT BLOCKS

b

DRAWER GUIDE

c

Construction

To avoid the difficulties of working inside the table frame more than necessary, the drawer supports are best completed on the bench and dropped in when assembled. Position two of the drawer runner support blocks on the bench, spaced the length of the drawer runner apart (fig. 25a). Apply glue to the edges facing uppermost, then lower and pin the drawer runner in place using two 25mm (1in) panel pins at each end (fig. 25a). Next stand the drawer guide on edge (fig. 25b), and run glue along the top edge. Turn the drawer runner with support blocks attached upside down and pin (fig. 25b), using 32mm (1¼in) panel pins. The completed runner will now appear as in fig. 25c. Repeat the same procedure with the other drawer support and put to one side to dry before fixing in the table frame.

Fig. 26

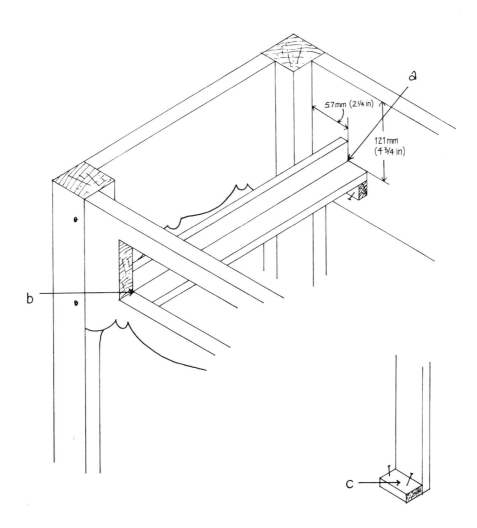

57mm (2¼ in)

121mm
(4¾ in)

a

b

c

Fixing

To obtain the correct position for fixing the drawer support to the table back, it is necessary to draw two lines at the locations shown in fig. 26a. The point at which they cross will be the inner corner of the drawer runner and drawer guide, the front end of the drawer support being positioned so that the drawer runner and drawer guide fit flush with the bottom and side edges of the drawer opening (fig. 26b). Stand the drawer supports on end and tap two 25mm (1in) panel pins into each block (fig. 26c), so that the tips of the pins just show through the back of the block. Smear a good covering of glue on both ends of the drawer supports and lower them into place. Tap home the panel pins and leave to dry. Repeat the same procedure with the other drawer support.

Fig. 27

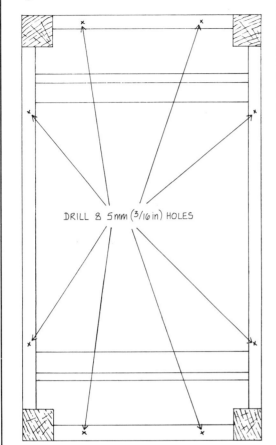

DRILL 8 5mm (3/16 in) HOLES

Fixing the top

To fix the top onto the table frame drill eight holes at the positions shown in fig. 27. The angle of the holes to be drilled and the fixing instructions are shown in fig. 16b, c and d. The table top should overhang the table frame about 32mm (1¼in) at the front and ends, and by about 6.4mm (¼in) at the back.

Drawer

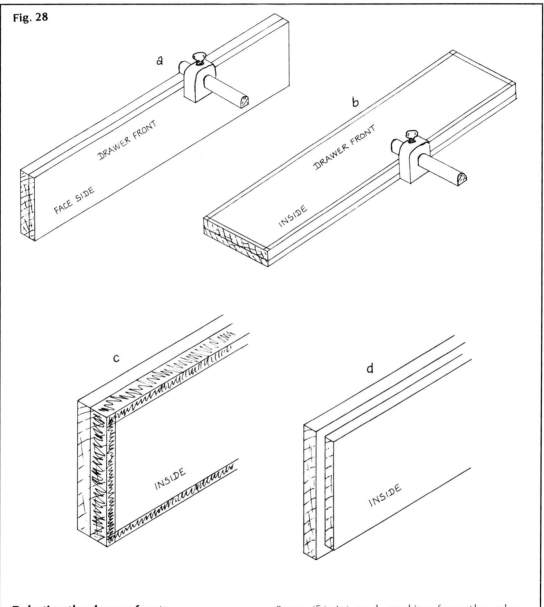

Fig. 28

Rebating the drawer fronts

The first stage of constructing the drawer is to form a rebate on the inside of the drawer front. Set a gauge to 9.5mm (³⁄₈in) and, working from the front (face side), gauge a line around all four edges (fig. 28a). Reset the gauge to 8mm (⁵⁄₁₆in) and, working from the edge, mark a line on the inside of the drawer front as shown in fig. 28b. The area between the gauge lines (shaded in fig. 28c), can now be cut away, leaving the finished rebate as shown in fig. 28d.

Fig. 29

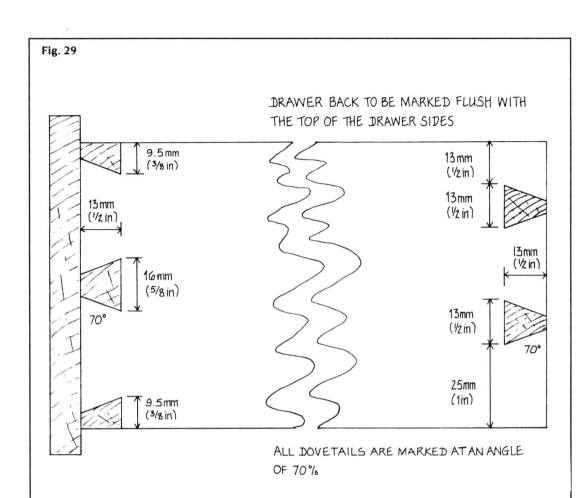

DRAWER BACK TO BE MARKED FLUSH WITH THE TOP OF THE DRAWER SIDES

9.5mm (³/₈ in)

13mm (¹/₂ in)

16mm (⁵/₈ in)

70°

9.5mm (³/₈ in)

13mm (¹/₂ in)

13mm (¹/₂ in)

13mm (¹/₂ in)

13mm (¹/₂ in)

70°

25mm (1in)

ALL DOVETAILS ARE MARKED AT AN ANGLE OF 70%

Dovetail joints

Next, mark and cut the dovetail joints, the sizes of which are shown in fig. 29. Details on how to make a dovetail joint can be found on *page* 130.

Fig. 30

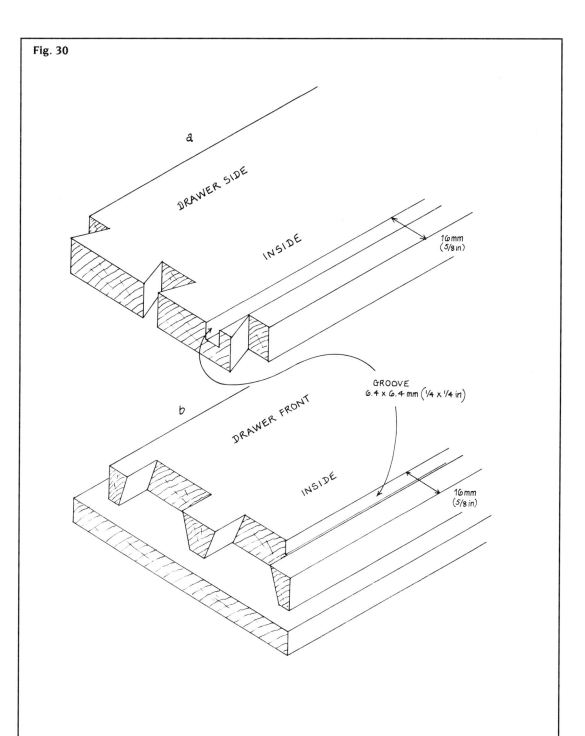

a

DRAWER SIDE

INSIDE

16mm
(5/8 in)

GROOVE
6.4 x 6.4 mm (¼ x ¼ in)

b

DRAWER FRONT

INSIDE

16mm
(5/8 in)

Groove to house drawer bottom

It is now necessary to make a groove 6.4 × 6.4mm (¼ × ¼in), 16mm (⅝in) up on the inside of both drawer sides (fig. 30a), and on the inside of the drawer front (fig. 30b), to house the drawer bottom.

Fig. 31

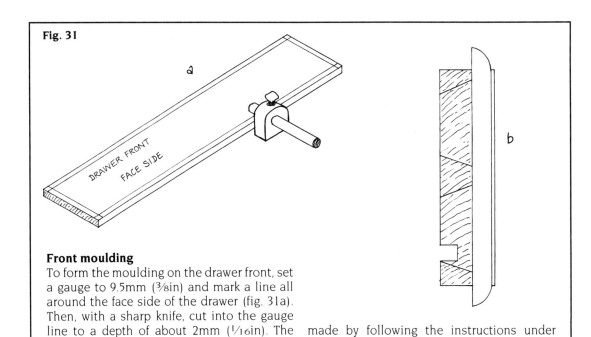

Front moulding

To form the moulding on the drawer front, set a gauge to 9.5mm (³⁄₈in) and mark a line all around the face side of the drawer (fig. 31a). Then, with a sharp knife, cut into the gauge line to a depth of about 2mm (¹⁄₁₆in). The completed moulding shown in fig. 31b can be made by following the instructions under Mouldings *page* 127.

Fig. 32

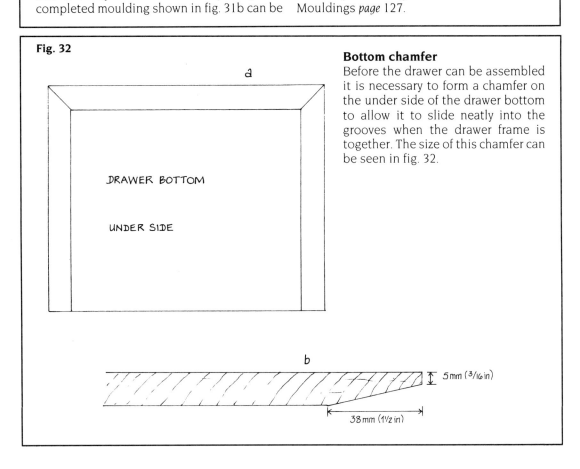

Bottom chamfer

Before the drawer can be assembled it is necessary to form a chamfer on the under side of the drawer bottom to allow it to slide neatly into the grooves when the drawer frame is together. The size of this chamfer can be seen in fig. 32.

Fig. 33

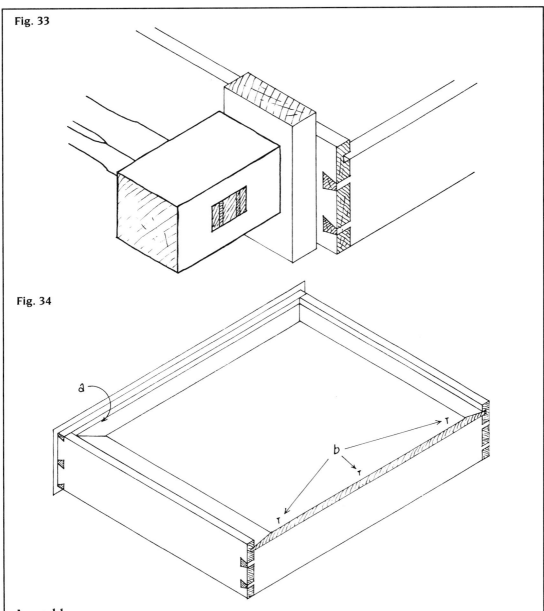

Fig. 34

Assembly

To assemble the drawer, apply a good smear of glue to all joints; then, with a block of wood and a mallet, tap the joints firmly together (fig. 33). Turn the drawer upside down and slide home the bottom, making quite sure that it goes well into the groove on the back of the drawer front (fig. 34a). Three 25mm (1in) panel pins should now be tapped through the drawer bottom into the back (fig. 34b), so

completing the drawer construction. The handles for the drawer are purely a matter of personal taste, but a wooden knob of a type that would suit this table is illustrated on *page 139.*

To complete the table sandpaper to a smooth finish and apply the polish or wax of your choice.

Refectory Table

Refectory tables, with their rails and stretchers tenoned into the legs, first appeared during the sixteenth century. Their massive tops sometimes measured 20 feet (6 metres) or more in length and needed six or eight legs to support them. Needless to say, this one is somewhat smaller, although you can easily build it larger if you want to and have the room.

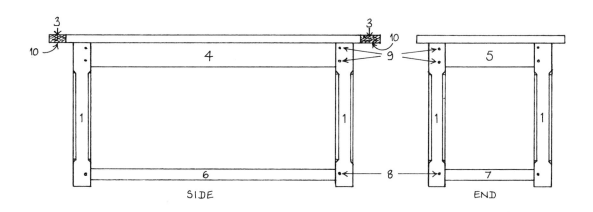

SIDE   END

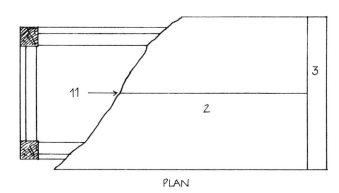

PLAN

Refectory table showing part numbers.
Top size: 1828 × 813mm (72 × 32in)
Height: 800mm (31½in)
Timber: elm
Finish: oak stain and varnish

MATERIALS

Part no.	Part name	No. of pieces	Size	
1	Legs	4	762 × 96 × 96mm	(30 × 3¾ × 3¾in)
2	Top	*	1828 × 813 × 38mm	(72 × 32 × 1½in)
3	Cleats for top ends	2	813 × 101 × 38mm	(32 × 4 × 1½in)
4	Top rails, side	2	1486 × 127 × 32mm	(58½ × 5 × 1¼in)
5	Top rails, end	2	609 × 127 × 32mm	(24 × 5 × 1¼in)
6	Stretchers, side	2	1511 × 96 × 64mm	(59½ × 3¾ × 2½in)
7	Stretchers, end	2	635 × 96 × 64mm	(25 × 3¾ × 2½in)
8	Dowel pegs, bottom joints	8	70 × 13mm	(2¾ × ½in)
9	Dowel pegs, top joints	16	45 × 13mm	(1¾ × ½in)
10	Dowel pegs, table top	8	32 × 13mm	(1¼ × ½in)
11	Plywood strip	†	1626 × 35 × 13mm	(64 × 1⅜ × ½in)

Wood glue
12 no. 10 steel countersunk screws, 51mm (2in)

* number depends on board widths available
† one for each join in the table top

CONSTRUCTION

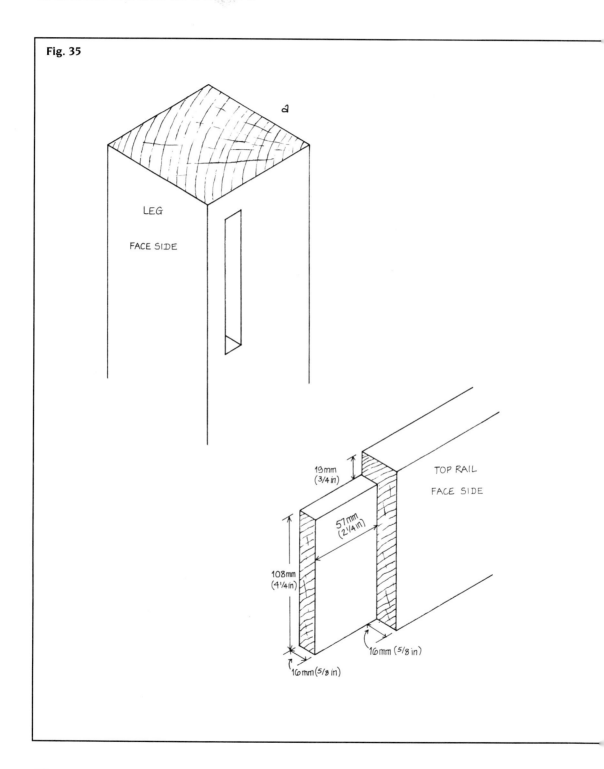

Fig. 35

LEG

FACE SIDE

TOP RAIL

FACE SIDE

19mm
(3/4 in)

57 mm
(2 1/4 in)

108mm
(4 1/4 in)

16mm (5/8 in)

16mm (5/8 in)

48

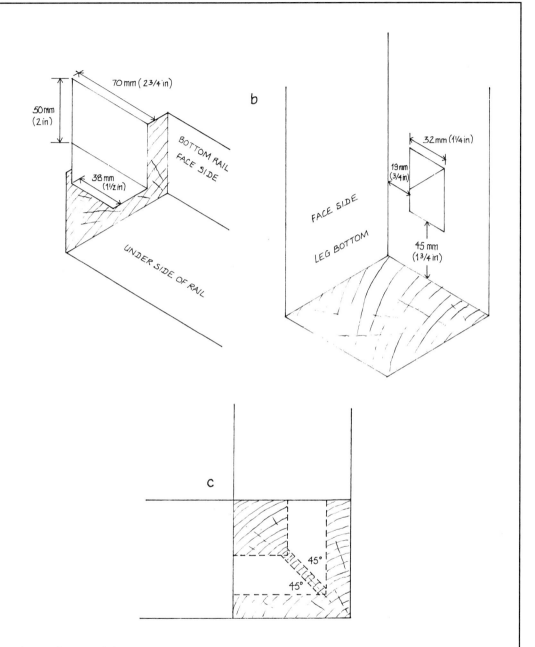

70 mm (2 3/4 in)

50 mm (2 in)

38 mm (1 1/2 in)

BOTTOM RAIL FACE SIDE

UNDER SIDE OF RAIL

b

32 mm (1 1/4 in)

19 mm (3/4 in)

45 mm (1 3/4 in)

FACE SIDE

LEG BOTTOM

c

45°

45°

Mortise and tenon joints

Once all the timber has been cut to size, the first operation is to mark and cut the mortise and tenon joints. The top joints are exactly the same size and one is illustrated in fig. 35a, which shows all the measurements required to make it. Fig. 35b shows one of the bottom joints. Again these are all identical, and the measurements needed to make them are also shown. Fig. 35c shows how the tenons will look once inserted into the leg mortise. For further details on making mortise and tenon joints see *page* 134.

Fig. 36

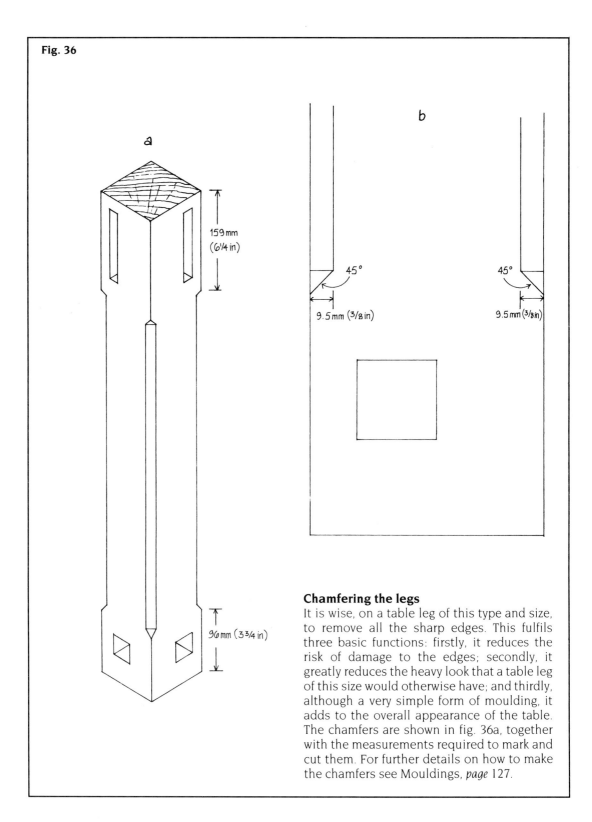

a

159 mm
(6¼ in)

96 mm (3¾ in)

b

45°

9.5 mm (3/8 in)

45°

9.5 mm (3/8 in)

Chamfering the legs

It is wise, on a table leg of this type and size, to remove all the sharp edges. This fulfils three basic functions: firstly, it reduces the risk of damage to the edges; secondly, it greatly reduces the heavy look that a table leg of this size would otherwise have; and thirdly, although a very simple form of moulding, it adds to the overall appearance of the table. The chamfers are shown in fig. 36a, together with the measurements required to mark and cut them. For further details on how to make the chamfers see Mouldings, *page* 127.

Fig. 37

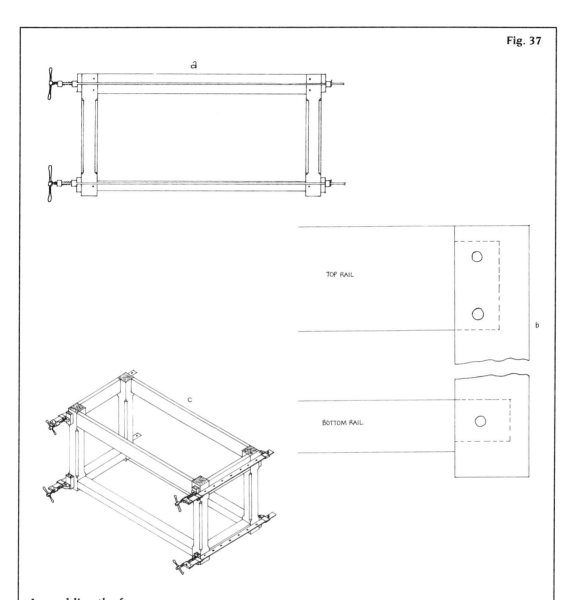

TOP RAIL

b

BOTTOM RAIL

a

c

Assembling the frame

As this is a large table, it is advisable to assemble the side sections first. Squeeze a generous amount of glue into the mortises which are to take the side rail and stretcher, push the legs onto the rail and stretcher and cramp up (fig. 37a). Next, drill two 13mm (½in) holes to a depth of about 45mm (1¾in) in each of the top joints and one 13mm (½in) hole to a depth of about 70mm (2¾in) in each of the bottom ones, at approximately the positions shown in fig. 37b.

Squeeze a blob of glue into each hole and tap home a peg in each. Remove the cramps and repeat the procedure with the other side. The remaining joints can now be glued and the end rails and end stretchers pushed into place. Cramp up as shown in fig. 37c. Drill, glue and peg the joints in the same way as the sides (fig. 37b). Wipe away any surplus glue from the joints and stand the frame to one side to dry for about 24 hours.

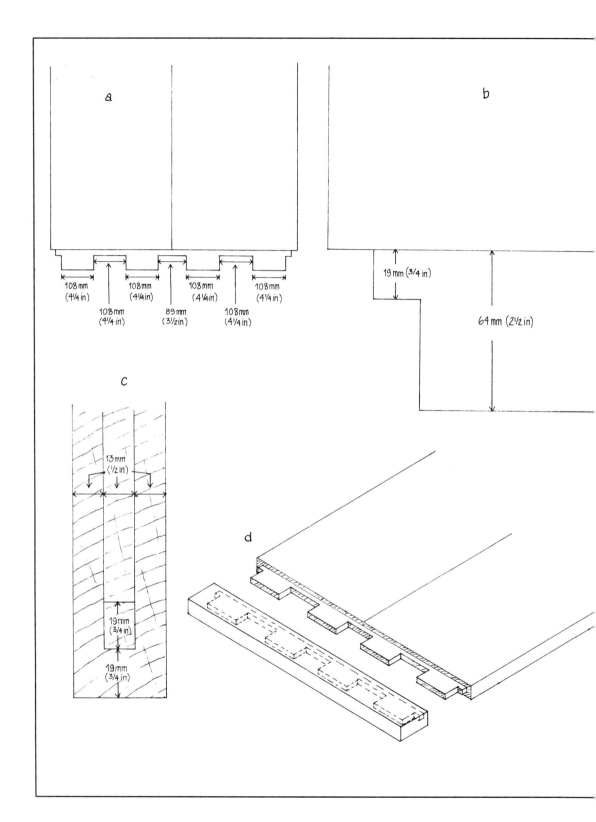

a

108 mm
(4¼ in)

108 mm
(4¼ in)

108mm
(4¼in)

108 mm
(4¼in)

108mm
(4¼ in)

89mm
(3½in)

108mm
(4¼in)

b

19 mm (3/4 in)

64 mm (2½ in)

c

13 mm
(½ in)

19mm
(3/4 in)

19mm
(3/4 in)

d

Fig. 38

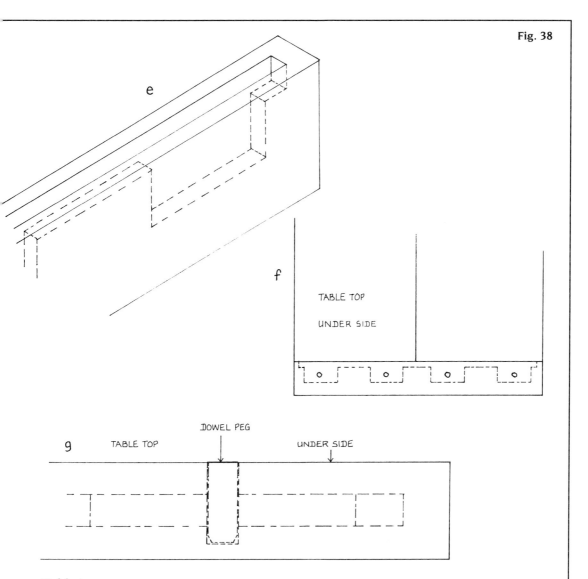

Table top

To form a table top of this size it will be necessary to join two, three or maybe four boards together. To do this, follow the instructions in Jointing Edge to Edge (*page* 136). When the desired width has been obtained (in this case 813mm – 32in), cleats must be applied to each end to prevent warping. A series of tenons must now be formed at each end of the top as shown in fig. 38a and enlarged in fig. 38b and c; the necessary measurements are also given in the diagram. The cleats must have corresponding mortises cut into them (fig. 38d and e). (See also Mortise and Tenon Joints, *page* 134.) When a snug fit has been obtained, glue the joints and tap them into position. Turn the table top onto its face and from the under side drill one 13mm (½in) hole into each joint to a depth of 32mm (1¼in) (fig. 38f and g). Squeeze a blob of glue into each hole and tap home the dowel pegs. Wipe away any surplus glue with a damp cloth and place the top to one side to dry thoroughly.

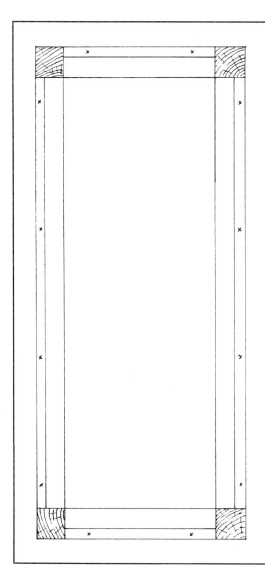

Fixing the top

To fix the top to the under frame drill 12 holes at the positions shown in fig. 39. The angle of the hole and the remainder of the fixing instructions are shown in fig. 16b, c and d.

To complete the table, sand it thoroughly and apply the finish of your choice.

Fig. 39

5 Box Stool

Box stools, although not often found in this form, are nevertheless a very useful addition to any household. The lid lifts to reveal a box compartment ideal for storage.

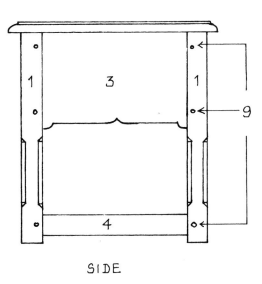

SIDE

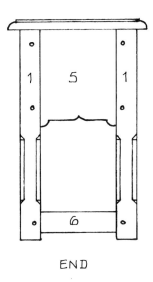

END

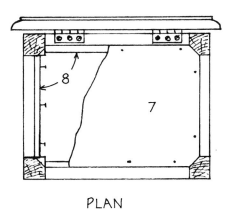

PLAN

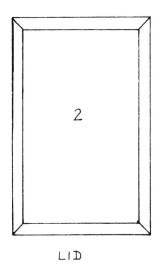

LID

Box stool showing part numbers.
Top size: 457 × 305mm (18 × 12in)
Height: 467mm (18⅜in)
Timber: oak
Finish: oak stain and varnish

MATERIALS

Part no.	Part name	No. of pieces	Size	
1	Legs	4	444 × 45 × 45mm	(17½ × 1¾ × 1¾in)
2	Top	1	457 × 305 × 22mm	(18 × 12 × ⅞in)
3	Sides	2	368 × 203 × 22mm	(14½ × 8 × ⅞in)
4	Bottom rails, side	2	368 × 45 × 22mm	(14½ × 1¾ × ⅞in)
5	Ends	2	216 × 203 × 22mm	(8½ × 8 × ⅞in)
6	Bottom rails, end	2	216 × 45 × 22mm	(8½ × 1¾ × ⅞in)
7	Stool bottom	1	362 × 210 × 13mm	(14¼ × 8¼ × ½in)
8	Bottom support battens	1	965 × 13 × 13mm	(38 × ½ × ½in)
9	Dowel pegs	24	32 × 6.4mm	(1¼ × ¼in)

Wood glue

1 pair of hinges, 64mm (2½in) × 19mm (¾in), and screws to fix

10 panel pins, 25mm (1in)

12 panel pins, 32mm (1¼in)

CONSTRUCTION

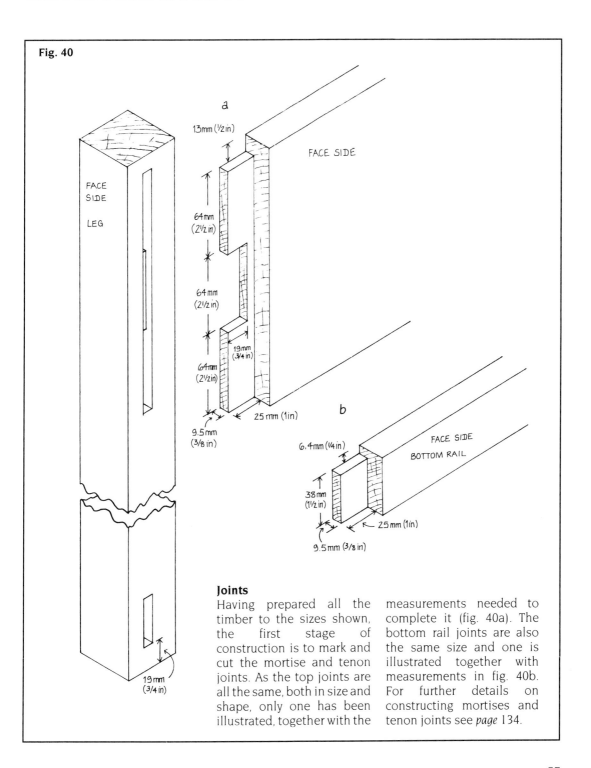

Fig. 40

a

13mm (½ in)

FACE SIDE

FACE SIDE

LEG

64mm
(2½ in)

64mm
(2½ in)

19mm
(3/4 in)

64mm
(2½in)

9.5mm
(3/8 in)

25 mm (1in)

b

6.4mm (¼ in)

FACE SIDE

BOTTOM RAIL

38 mm
(1½ in)

25 mm (1in)

9.5mm (3/8 in)

19 mm
(3/4 in)

Joints

Having prepared all the timber to the sizes shown, the first stage of construction is to mark and cut the mortise and tenon joints. As the top joints are all the same, both in size and shape, only one has been illustrated, together with the measurements needed to complete it (fig. 40a). The bottom rail joints are also the same size and one is illustrated together with measurements in fig. 40b. For further details on constructing mortises and tenon joints see *page* 134.

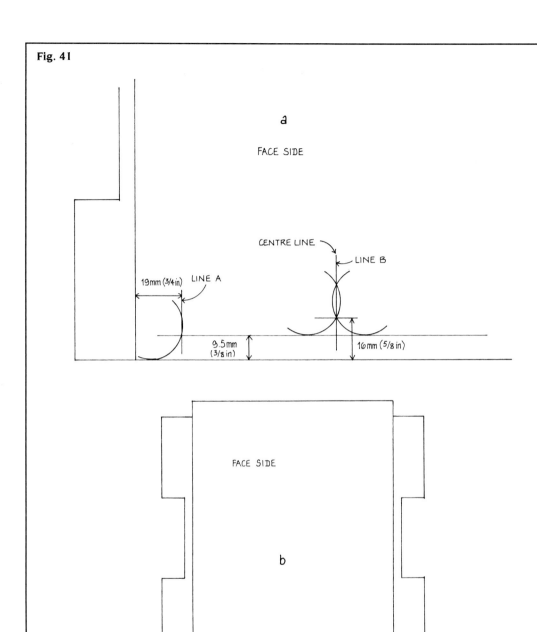

Fig. 41

a

FACE SIDE

CENTRE LINE

LINE B

19mm (3/4 in)   LINE A

9.5mm (3/8 in)   16mm (5/8 in)

FACE SIDE

b

Shaping the ends and sides

To form the shaping on the under frame (fig. 41b), mark out the ends using the measurements shown in fig. 41a. The sides can be marked using the same measurements, although the distance between line A and line B will be greater. Once the pieces have been marked, cramp the timber in a vice and cut out the shape with a coping saw. Any roughness made with the saw blade can be removed by sandpapering.

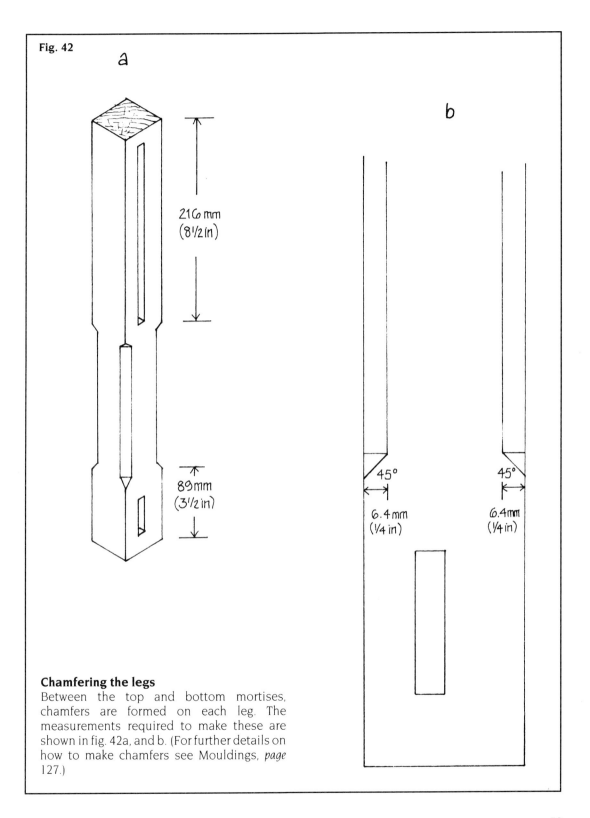

Fig. 42

a

216 mm
(8½ in)

89mm
(3½ in)

b

45°

45°

6.4 mm
(¼ in)

6.4mm
(¼ in)

Chamfering the legs

Between the top and bottom mortises, chamfers are formed on each leg. The measurements required to make these are shown in fig. 42a, and b. (For further details on how to make chamfers see Mouldings, *page* 127.)

Fig. 43

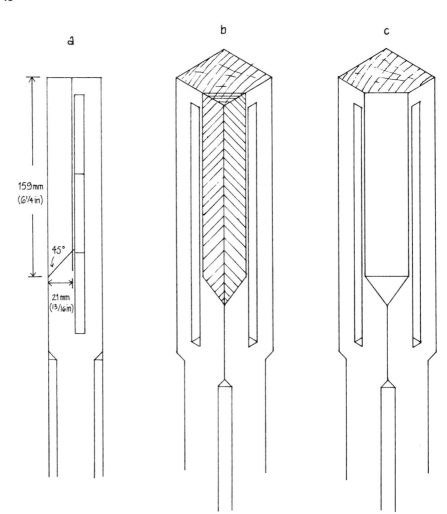

a

159mm
(6¼in)

45°

21mm
(¹³/₁₆in)

b

c

Chamfering the leg tops

The last task before assembling the stool is to remove the sharp inside edge from the top of each leg. Mark out each leg using the measurements shown in fig. 43a. The shaded area in fig. 43b can now be cut away with a panel saw, leaving the desired chamfer (fig. 43c). Any roughness remaining after sawing can be removed by sandpapering.

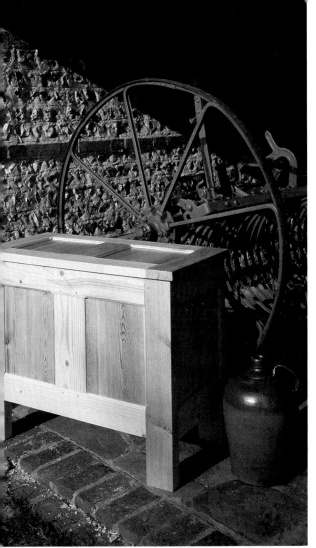

1 The panelled chest illustrated here has been constructed of pine because it is the easiest wood to obtain and is probably also the cheapest

2 The cricket table has been constructed of English elm, lightly stained to bring out the grain, and then polished

3 The side table shown here has been made of brown oak, then waxed using a good furniture wax to bring out the natural colour of the wood

4 The refectory table is constructed of English elm and has been treated with a hard varnish to withstand the punishment of everyday use

5 This particular box stool has been constructed of brown oak and waxed to enhance the rich beauty of the wood

6 The dresser has been constructed of English oak, then stained and polished

7 English oak was used for this cupboard, and was then lightly stained, polished and waxed

8 The joint stool has been made of English yew and the finish obtained simply by waxing with a good furniture wax

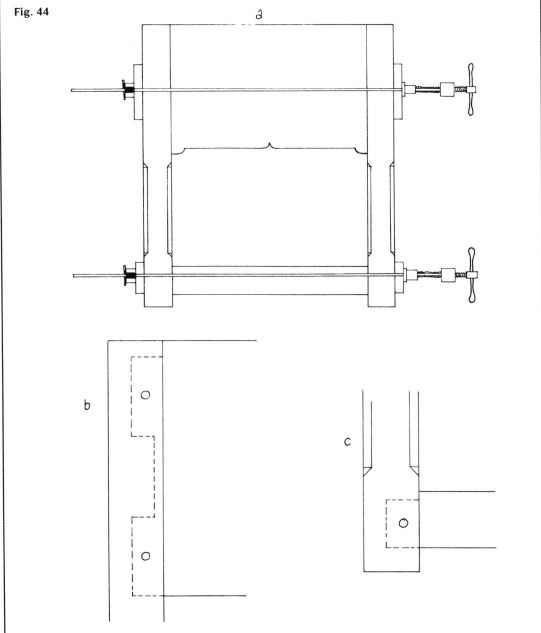

Fig. 44

Assembly

Squeeze a good coating of glue into each of the mortises that are to house the side rails, top and bottom. Push the tenons into their corresponding mortises and cramp up (fig. 44a). Drill two 6.4mm (¼in) holes in each of the top joints at the approximate positions shown in fig. 44b and one 6.4mm (¼in) hole at the position shown in fig. 44c. All holes should be drilled to a depth of about 35mm (1⅜in). Squeeze a blob of glue into each hole and tap home a dowel peg; wipe away any surplus glue with a damp cloth and remove the cramps.

Fig. 45

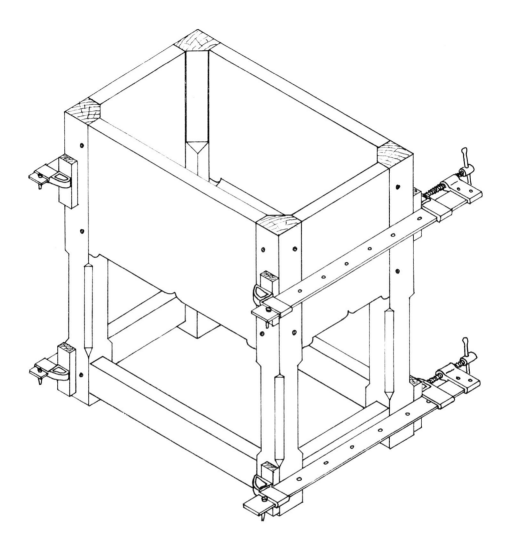

The remaining mortises can now be glued and the end, top and bottom rails pushed into position and cramped up (fig. 45). Drill and peg, using the same positions as for gluing up the sides (fig. 44b and c). Wipe away any surplus glue, remove the cramps and place to one side to dry for about 24 hours.

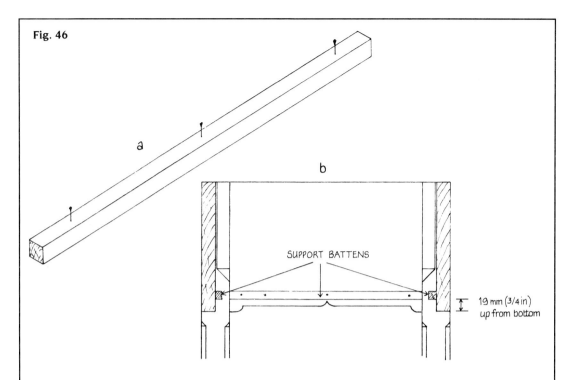

Fig. 46

SUPPORT BATTENS

19 mm (3/4 in)
up from bottom

Fixing the bottom support battens
Cut the bottom support battens into four pieces: two pieces 318mm (12½in) to fix to the side, and two pieces 165mm (6½in) to fix to the ends. Tap three 32mm (1¼in) panel pins in each batten (fig 46a), so that the tips of the pins just come through the batten. Smear a layer of glue along the inner edge, place into position as shown in fig. 46b and tap home the pins.

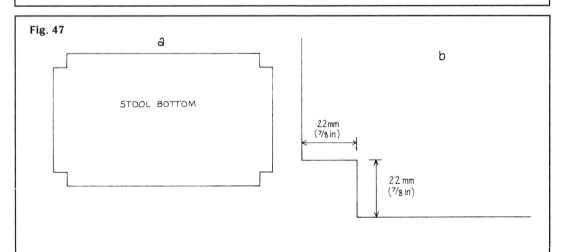

Fig. 47

STOOL BOTTOM

22mm (7/8 in)

22 mm (7/8 in)

Fixing the bottom
Before the stool bottom can be lowered into position a section from each corner must be removed (fig. 47). When this has been done, lower the bottom into position and pin using the 25mm (1in) panel pins.

Fig. 48

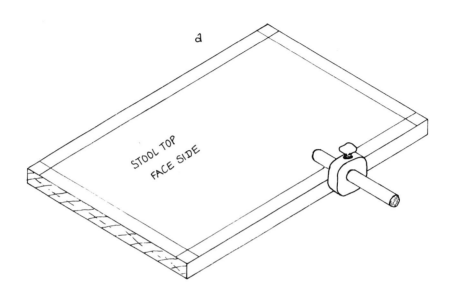

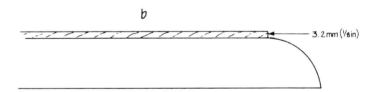

b

3.2mm (⅛in)

Stool top

To form the moulding around the stool top, set a gauge to 22mm (⅞in) and, from the outer edge, mark a line all around on the top (fig. 48a). With a Stanley knife or similar sharp knife, cut into the gauge line to a depth of almost 3.2mm (⅛in) to complete the moulding as shown in fig. 48b. (See also Mouldings, *page* 127.)

Fig. 49

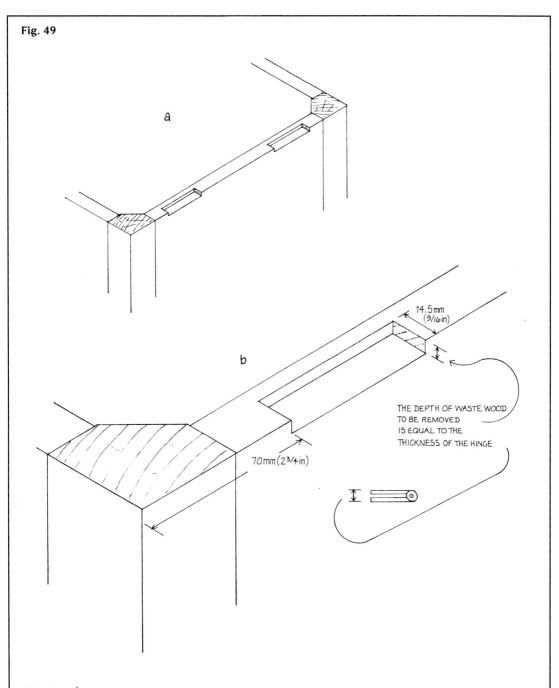

a

14.5mm
(9/16in)

b

THE DEPTH OF WASTE WOOD
TO BE REMOVED
IS EQUAL TO THE
THICKNESS OF THE HINGE

70mm (2³/4in)

Hinging the top

Fig. 49 shows the positions and amount of waste wood to be removed in order to house the hinge size stated. If, for any reason, your hinge size differs from the one given, then the housing must be altered accordingly. For more detail on removing the waste from the hinge housing, refer to fig. 10.

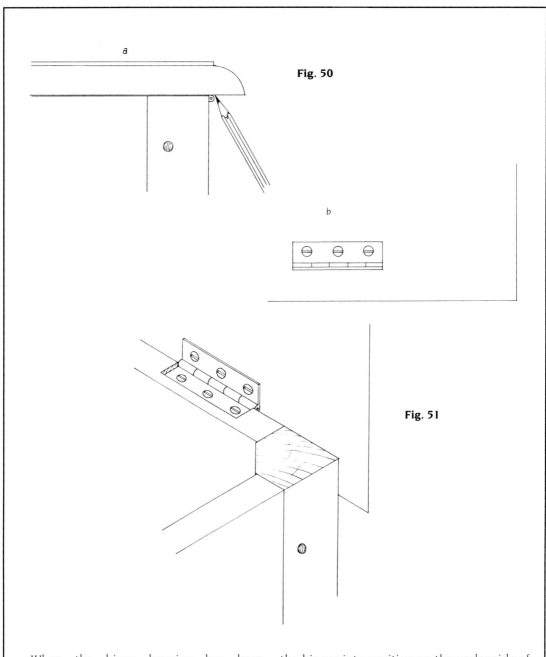

Fig. 50

Fig. 51

When the hinge housing has been completed, rest the hinges into it, but at this stage do not fix them. Place the top on the frame so that there is an even overhang of 25mm (1in) all around, and mark the hinge positions on the under side of the top with a pencil (fig. 50a). Remove the top and screw the hinges into position on the under side of the top first (fig. 50b), then onto the stool frame (fig. 51).

The stool can now be sanded and the finish of your choice applied.

⑥ Dresser

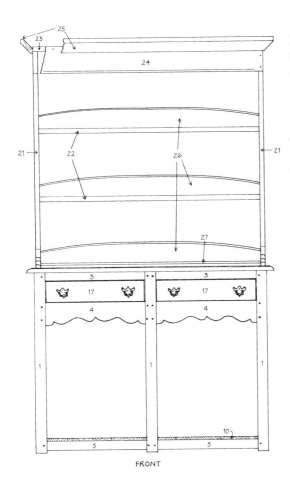

FRONT

Dresser showing part numbers.
Dresser base top size:
1218 × 457mm (48 × 18in)
Height of dresser:
1991mm (78⅜in)
Timber: oak
Finish: oak stain and varnish

END

PLAN

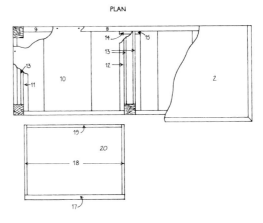

It was probably in the seventeenth century that the dresser gained its shelves, making it the piece of furniture we all recognise today. Although usually made of oak, the design, shape and size could differ enormously. This was due to the area in which it was made and the quantity of crockery and kitchen items it had to house.

MATERIALS

Part no.	Part name	No. of pieces	Size	
1	Legs	5	863 × 50 × 50mm	(34 × 2 × 2in)
2	Top	*	1218 × 457 × 22mm	(48 × 18 × $^7/_8$in)
3	Front rails, top	2	546 × 38 × 22mm	(21$^1/_2$ × 1$^1/_2$ × $^7/_8$in)
4	Front rails, middle	2	546 × 114 × 22mm	(21$^1/_2$ × 4$^1/_2$ × $^7/_8$in)
5	Front rails, bottom	2	546 × 45 × 22mm	(21$^1/_2$ × 1$^3/_4$ × $^7/_8$in)
6	End rails, top	2	375 × 254 × 22mm	(14$^3/_4$ × 10 × $^7/_8$in)
7	End rails, bottom	2	375 × 45 × 22mm	(14$^3/_4$ × 1$^3/_4$ × $^7/_8$in)
8	Back rail, top	1	1092 × 254 × 22mm	(43 × 10 × $^7/_8$in)
9	Back rail, bottom	1	1092 × 45 × 22mm	(43 × 1$^3/_4$ × $^7/_8$in)
10	Pot board	*	1144 × 426 × 13mm	(45 × 16$^3/_4$ × $^1/_2$in)
11	Drawer supports, end	2	381 × 50 × 13mm	(15 × 2 × $^1/_2$in)
12	Drawer support, middle	1	381 × 101 × 13mm	(15 × 4 × $^1/_2$in)
13	Drawer guides, end	2	324 × 38 × 13mm	(12$^3/_4$ × 1$^1/_2$ × $^1/_2$in)
	Drawer guides, middle	2	352 × 38 × 13mm	(13$^7/_8$ × 1$^1/_2$ × $^1/_2$in)
14	Drawer runner support block	1	101 × 25 × 13mm	(4 × 1 × $^1/_2$in)
15	Drawer stop blocks	4	size determined after drawers have been fitted	
16	Dowel pegs	34	32 × 6.4mm	(1$^1/_4$ × $^1/_4$in)

Drawer parts for two drawers

17	Drawer fronts	2	495 × 101 × 22mm	(19$^1/_2$ × 4 × $^7/_8$in)
18	Drawer sides	4	343 × 101 × 13mm	(13$^1/_2$ × 4 × $^1/_2$in)
19	Drawer backs	2	495 × 83 × 13mm	(19$^1/_2$ × 3$^1/_4$ × $^1/_2$in)
20	Drawer bottoms	2*	483 × 343 × 13mm	(19 × 13$^1/_2$ × $^1/_2$in)
	Knobs (if required)	4	76 × 50 × 50mm	(3 × 2 × 2in)

Dresser rack

21	Sides	2	1003 × 152 × 22mm	(39$^1/_2$ × 6 × $^7/_8$in)
22	Shelves	2	1117 × 140 × 22mm	(44 × 5$^1/_2$ × $^7/_8$in)
23	Top	1	1143 × 140 × 22mm	(45 × 5$^1/_2$ × $^7/_8$in)
24	Pelmet	1	1143 × 149 × 13mm	(45 × 5$^7/_8$ × $^1/_2$in)
25	Moulding	1	1676 × 76 × 22mm	(66 × 3 × $^7/_8$in)
26	Shelf backing	3	1117 × 114 × 13mm	(44 × 4$^1/_2$ × $^1/_2$in)
27	Bottom strengthening rung	1	1092 × 22 × 22mm	(43 × $^7/_8$ × $^7/_8$in)
28	Rack shoes	2	356 × 89 × 22mm	(14 × 3$^1/_2$ × $^7/_8$in)
29	Dowel pegs	4	22 × 6.4mm	($^7/_8$ × $^1/_4$in)

Wood glue
Lost head nails, 64mm (2½in)
Panel pins, 50mm (2in)
Panel pins, 38mm (1½in)
Panel pins, 32mm (1¼in)
Panel pins, 25mm (1in)
2 no. 8 steel countersunk screws, 25mm (1in)
12 no. 8 steel countersunk screws, 38mm (1½in)

* number depends on board widths available

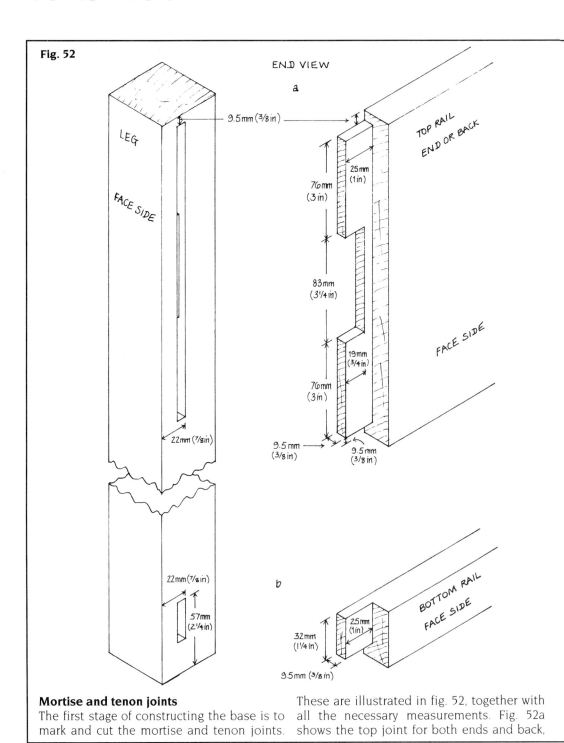

Fig. 52

END VIEW

a

9.5mm (3/8in)

LEG

FACE SIDE

22mm (7/8in)

TOP RAIL
END OR BACK

25mm (1in)

76mm (3in)

83mm (3¼in)

19mm (3/4in)

76mm (3in)

FACE SIDE

9.5mm (3/8in)

9.5mm (3/8in)

22mm (7/8in)

57mm (2¼in)

b

BOTTOM RAIL
FACE SIDE

25mm (1in)

32mm (1¼in)

9.5mm (3/8in)

Mortise and tenon joints

The first stage of constructing the base is to mark and cut the mortise and tenon joints. These are illustrated in fig. 52, together with all the necessary measurements. Fig. 52a shows the top joint for both ends and back,

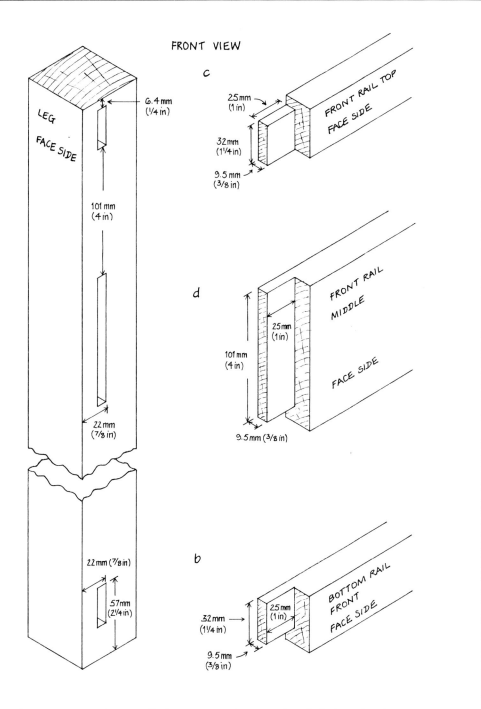

FRONT VIEW

LEG
FACE SIDE

6.4 mm
(1/4 in)

101 mm
(4 in)

22 mm
(7/8 in)

22 mm (7/8 in)

57mm
(21/4 in)

c

25 mm
(1 in)

FRONT RAIL TOP
FACE SIDE

32 mm
(11/4 in)

9.5 mm
(3/8 in)

d

FRONT RAIL
MIDDLE

25 mm
(1 in)

101 mm
(4 in)

FACE SIDE

9.5 mm (3/8 in)

b

BOTTOM RAIL
FRONT
FACE SIDE

25 mm
(1 in)

32 mm
(11/4 in)

9.5 mm
(3/8 in)

fig. 52b the joint used on all bottom stretchers, fig. 52c the joint used on the two top rails, and fig. 52d the joint on the two front rails immediately below the drawer opening. (See also Mortise and Tenon Joints, *page* 134.)

71

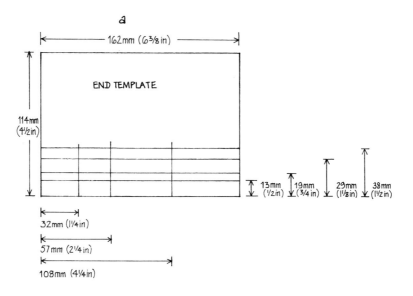

a

162mm (6⅜in)

END TEMPLATE

114mm
(4½in)

13mm   19mm   29mm   38mm
(½in)   (¾in)   (1⅛in) (1½in)

32mm (1¼in)

57mm (2¼in)

108mm (4¼in)

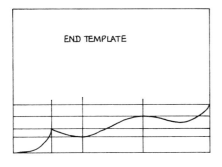

END TEMPLATE

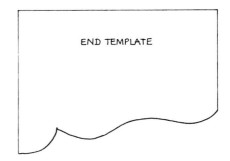

END TEMPLATE

Shaping the under frame

To create the shaping which appears below the drawer front opening and at each end of the dresser base, it is first necessary to make cardboard templates. These are made exactly half the width of the shaped rail, so the template has to be reversed to create the complete shape on each rail. Fig. 53a shows the template for each end and fig. 53b the template for the front rails. (For further details, see fig. 20.) The completed shape for the front and side rails is shown in fig. 53c.

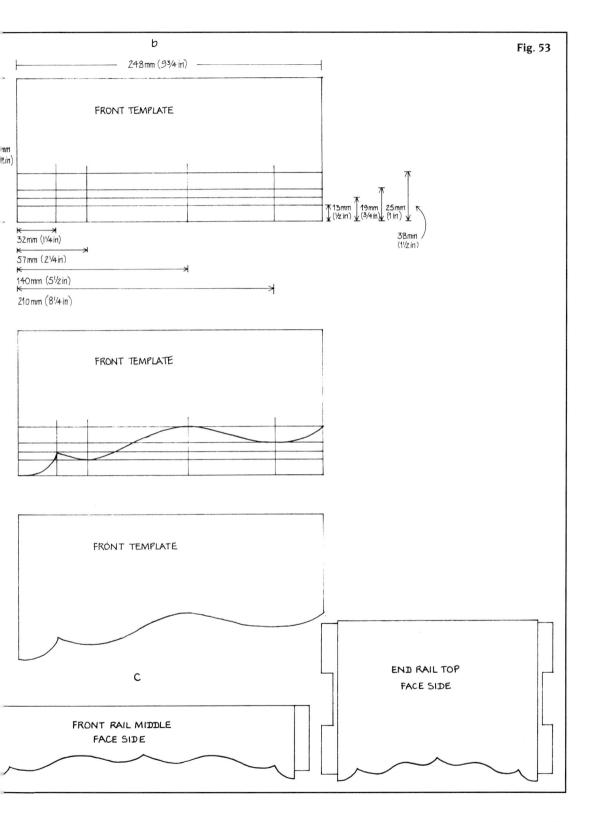

b

Fig. 53

248mm (9¾ in)

FRONT TEMPLATE

mm
in)

13mm 19mm 25mm
(½in) (¾in) (1in)

38mm
(1½in)

32mm (1¼in)

57mm (2¼in)

140mm (5½in)

210mm (8¼in)

FRONT TEMPLATE

FRONT TEMPLATE

c

END RAIL TOP
FACE SIDE

FRONT RAIL MIDDLE
FACE SIDE

Frame

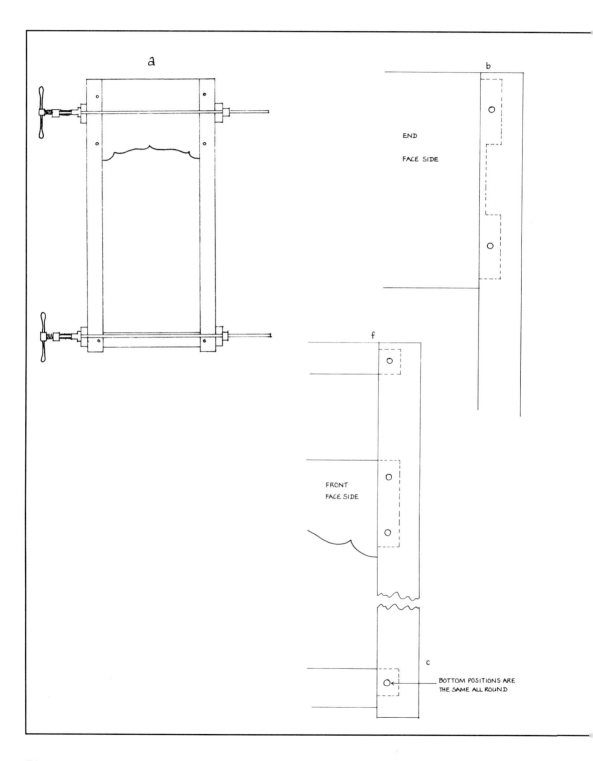

a

b

END

FACE SIDE

f

FRONT
FACE SIDE

c

BOTTOM POSITIONS ARE
THE SAME ALL ROUND

Fig. 54

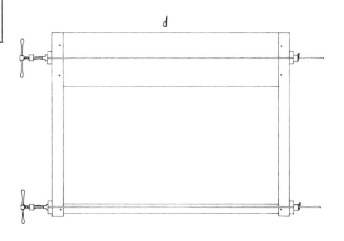

d

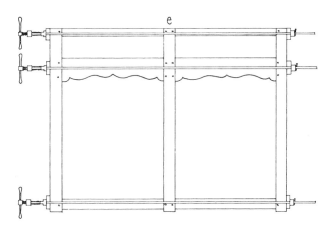

e

Assembling the frame

Having made quite sure that all joints fit, you can begin the first stage of assembly, starting with the ends. Squeeze a generous amount of glue into the mortises that are to take the top end rail and the bottom end stretcher, place these in position, and cramp up as shown in fig. 54a. Drill two 6mm (¼in) holes in each of the top joints and one in each of the bottom joints, at the approximate positions shown in fig. 54b and c, to a depth of about 32mm (1¼in). Squeeze a blob of glue in each hole and tap in one of the dowel pegs. Wipe away any surplus glue, then place to one side to dry. Repeat the same procedure with the other end.

When the ends are dry, the front and back pieces can be assembled. Squeeze glue into all remaining mortises and push home the pieces into their appropriate positions. Fig. 54d shows the back section and fig. 54e the front. Cramp up securely.

In the top joint of the rail, drill two holes 6.4mm (¼in) deep at the positions shown in fig. 54b and one in each of the bottom stretcher joints (fig. 54c). On the front section, using the same diameter drill, drill holes at the locations shown in fig. 54f and c. Squeeze a blob of glue into each hole, tap a dowel peg in each and wipe away any surplus glue. Then stand the frame to one side to dry for about 24 hours.

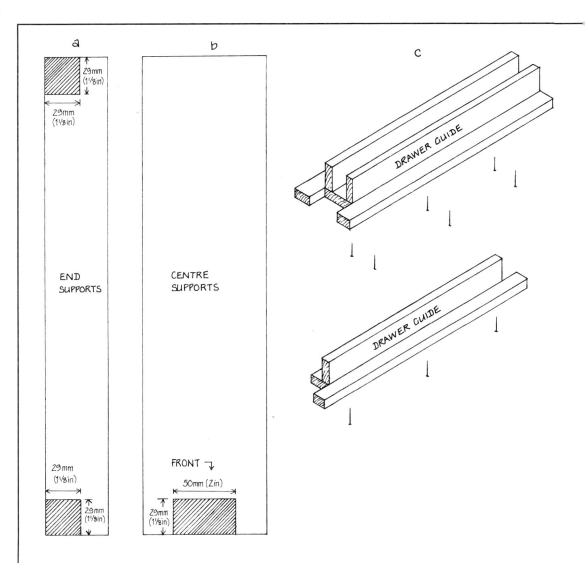

a

29mm
(1⅛in)

29mm
(1⅛in)

b

END
SUPPORTS

CENTRE
SUPPORTS

c

DRAWER GUIDE

DRAWER GUIDE

29mm
(1⅛in)

29mm
(1⅛in)

FRONT

50mm (2in)

29mm
(1⅛in)

Drawer supports and guides

Fig. 55a shows one of the end supports and fig. 55b the centre support. Using the measurements shown, mark and cut out the shaded area. On one long edge of each drawer guide, smear a layer of glue; place the drawer guides onto the drawer runners as shown in fig. 55c and fix using three 32mm (1¼in) panel pins in each. To insert the two end drawer supports into their correct positions (fig. 55d), glue the parts that come into into contact with the frame and lower into the position shown, using two 50mm (2in) panel pins.

Before the centre drawer support can be fixed it is necessary to fix the drawer runner support block to the back. Drill two holes about 5mm (³⁄₁₆in) in diameter in the support block at the positions shown in fig. 55e, and countersink. Smear a layer of glue onto the back of the block, and using two 25mm (1in) steel countersunk screws, fix at the position shown in fig. 55f. The centre drawer support can now be glued and lowered into position (fig. 55g), and fixed using two 50mm (2in) panel pins in the front, and two 25 mm (1in) panel pins in the back; take care to avoid the screws.

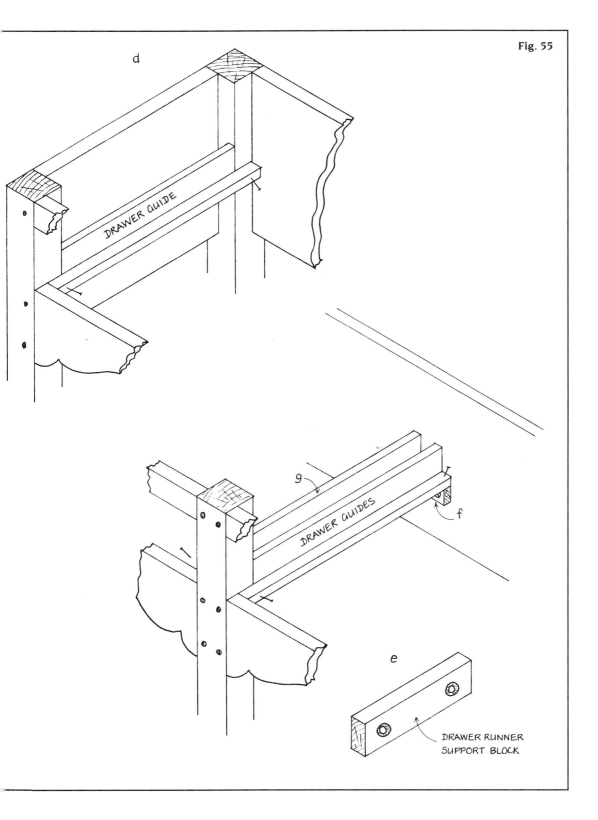

Fig. 55

d

DRAWER GUIDE

9

DRAWER GUIDES

f

e

DRAWER RUNNER
SUPPORT BLOCK

77

Fig. 56

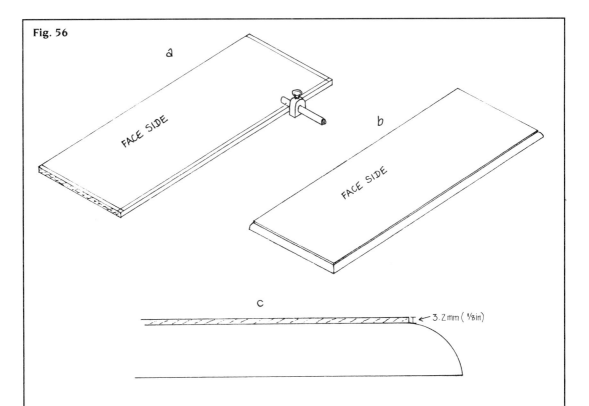

a

FACE SIDE

b

FACE SIDE

c

3.2mm (⅛in)

Making the top

When the top size has been obtained, either by buying a single plank or by gluing together two or three individual boards to make up the width, the next task is to form the moulding which runs along the front edge and returns along both ends. Set a gauge to 22mm (⅞in) and from the edge mark a line along the front and two ends on the top (fig. 56a), to form the remainder of the moulding as illustrated in fig. 56b and c. (See Mouldings, *page* 127.)

Fig. 57

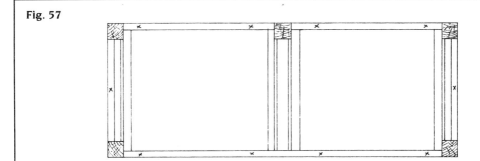

Fixing the top

To fix the top onto the dresser base, drill ten holes at the positions shown in fig. 57. The angle of the hole to be drilled and the fixing instructions are shown in figs. 16b, c and d. Allow the top to overhang the back of the base by about 6.4mm (¼in) and fix when the overhangs at each end are equal.

Fig. 58

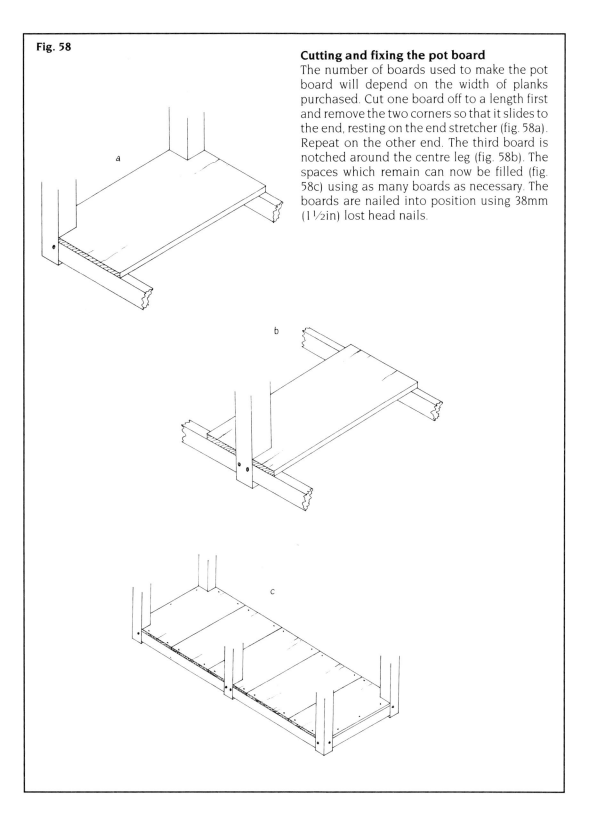

Cutting and fixing the pot board

The number of boards used to make the pot board will depend on the width of planks purchased. Cut one board off to a length first and remove the two corners so that it slides to the end, resting on the end stretcher (fig. 58a). Repeat on the other end. The third board is notched around the centre leg (fig. 58b). The spaces which remain can now be filled (fig. 58c) using as many boards as necessary. The boards are nailed into position using 38mm (1½in) lost head nails.

Drawers

Fig. 59

a

TOP EDGE

16mm
(5/8in)

70°

DRAWER

SIDE

16mm
(5/8in)

16mm
(5/8in)

13mm
(1/2in)

13mm
(1/2in)

75°

13mm
(1/2in)

38mm
(1½in)

13mm
(1/2in)

13mm
(1/2in)

FRONT TAILS 70°
BACK TAILS 75°

Dovetail joints

Both drawers are made in the same way. Having prepared all the drawer parts to the sizes required, the first stage of construction is to make the dovetail joints. These are illustrated in fig. 59a, b and c, together with all the necessary measurements. (For further information on forming dovetail joints see *page* 130.)

Groove to take the drawer bottom

It is now necessary to form a groove to hold the drawer bottom in position. This groove is illustrated in fig. 59b and c, together with the measurements needed to make it.

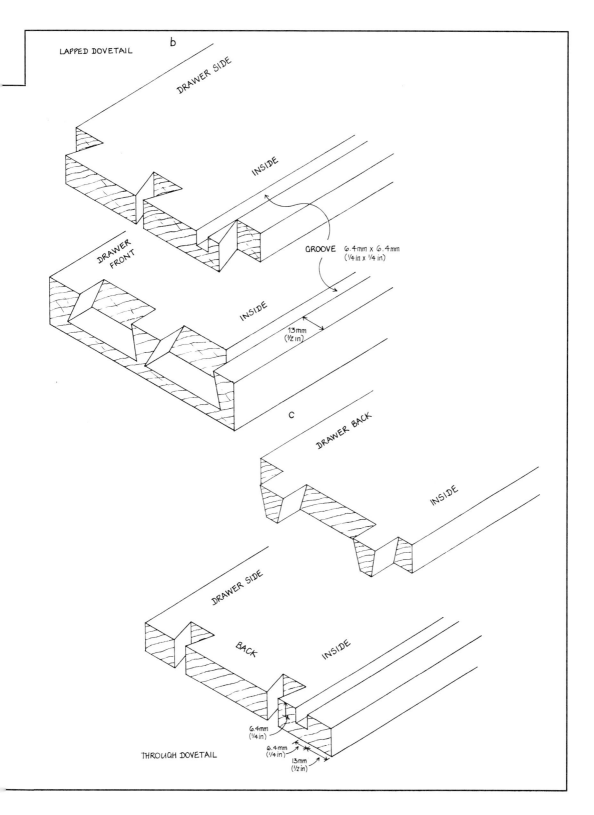

LAPPED DOVETAIL

b

DRAWER SIDE

INSIDE

DRAWER FRONT

INSIDE

GROOVE 6.4mm x 6.4mm
(¼ in x ¼ in)

13mm
(½ in)

c

DRAWER BACK

INSIDE

DRAWER SIDE

BACK

INSIDE

6.4mm
(¼ in)

6.4mm
(¼ in)

13mm
(½ in)

THROUGH DOVETAIL

Fig. 60

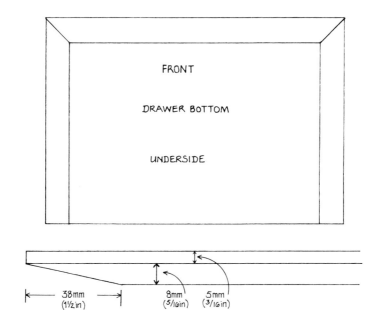

FRONT

DRAWER BOTTOM

UNDERSIDE

38mm
(1½in)

8mm
(5/16in)

5mm
(3/16in)

Drawer bottom

To enable the drawer bottom to slide into the drawer frame, form a chamfer on three sides of the drawer bottom. This is shown in fig. 60 with the measurements indicating the area which is to be planed away.

Fig. 61

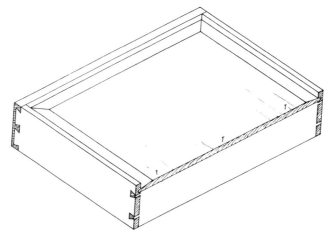

Assembly

To assemble the drawer, smear a generous amount of glue onto all joints and push the drawer frame firmly together. Slide the drawer bottom into position, ensuring that it goes well into the groove on the back of the drawer front, and secure using three 25mm (1in) panel pins (fig. 61). The drawers can now slide into place in the base until the fronts finish flush with the frame. To stop the drawers going any further into the dresser, glue and pin blocks onto the back of the drawer runners. Two blocks for each drawer will keep the drawer flush with the front. The handles for this dresser are a matter of personal taste, but a wooden knob of a suitable type is illustrated on *page* 139.

Rack

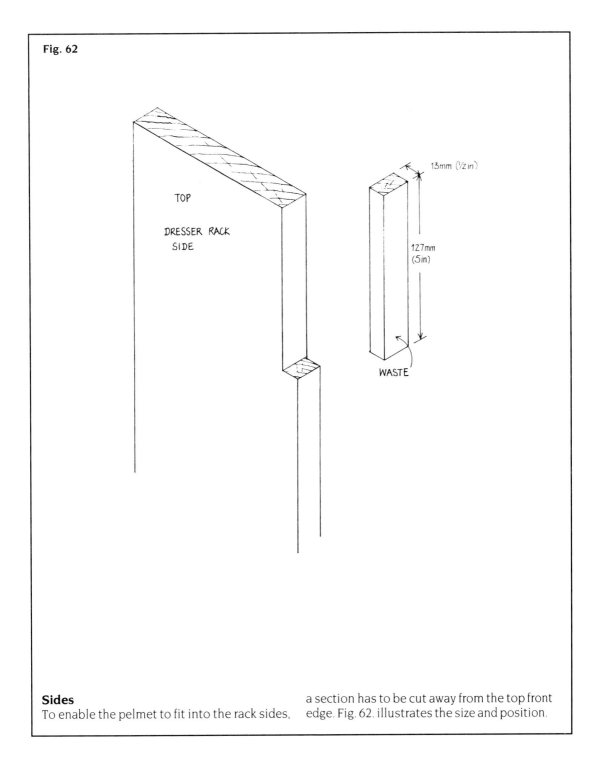

Fig. 62

TOP

DRESSER RACK
SIDE

13mm (½ in)

127mm
(5in)

WASTE

Sides
To enable the pelmet to fit into the rack sides, a section has to be cut away from the top front edge. Fig. 62. illustrates the size and position.

Fig. 63

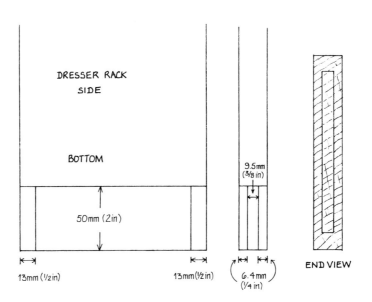

DRESSER RACK
SIDE

BOTTOM

50mm (2in)

13mm (½in)   13mm(½in)

9.5mm
(3/8 in)

6.4mm
(¼ in)

END VIEW

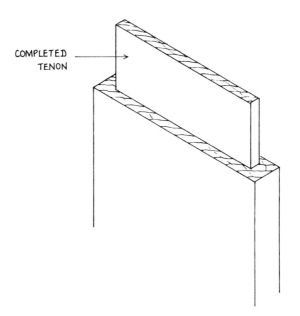

COMPLETED
TENON

Tenon

The tenon joint which has to be cut on the bottom of both side pieces, together with the measurements needed to make it, are shown in fig. 63. This tenon will eventually fit into a shoe which stops the rack from tipping forward.

Fig. 66

Fig. 64

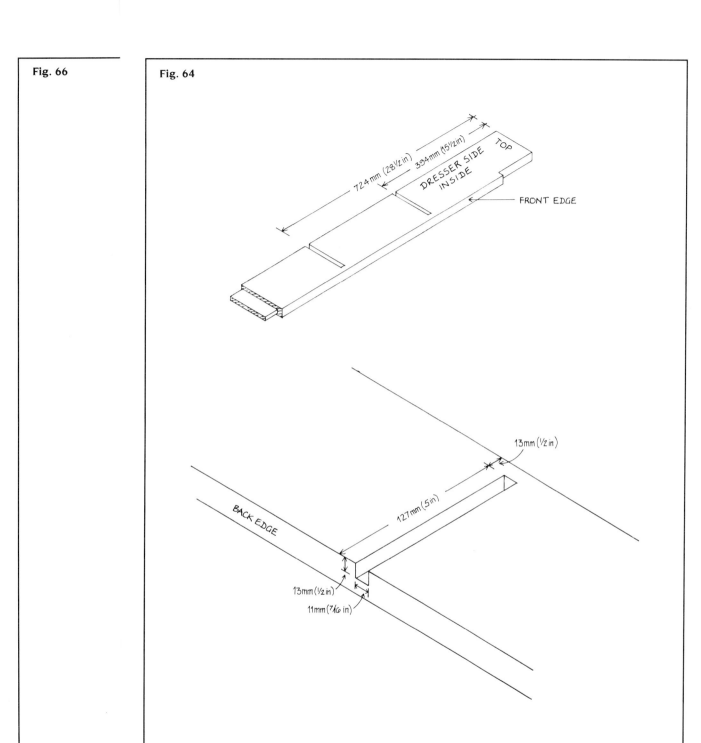

724 mm (28½ in)

394 mm (15½ in)

DRESSER SIDE INSIDE

TOP

FRONT EDGE

13 mm (½ in)

BACK EDGE

127 mm (5 in)

13 mm (½ in)

11 mm (7/16 in)

Making the tem
on the front of th
make a cardboal
of making this t

Groove to house shelves

On the inside of both side pieces two grooves
have now to be cut. Fig. 64 shows the size and
location of the grooves, together with the
necessary measurements.

Fig. 6

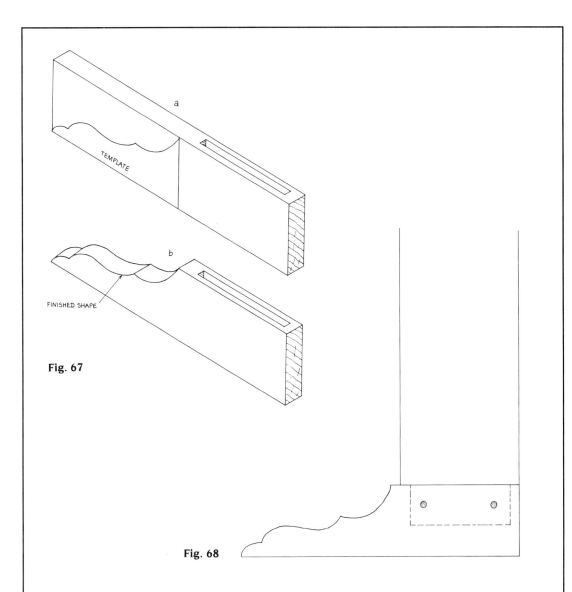

Fig. 67

Fig. 68

Marking and cutting   Lay the template on the shoe in the position shown in fig. 67a and mark around the shaped section with a pencil. Remove the template, and place it on the other side and again mark with a pencil. The shoe can now be cramped in a vice and the shape cut out using a coping saw (fig. 67b). Repeat on the other shoe and remove any roughness made by the saw by sanding with a medium glasspaper.

Fixing   To attach the shoes to the rack sides, squeeze a generous amount of glue into the mortises and push the shoes firmly into position (fig. 68). If the joint is somewhat loose, it is advisable to cramp it before drilling at the positions shown (fig. 68). Drill two 6.4mm (¼in) holes in each joint so that the holes go completely through the thickness of the shoe. Squeeze a blob of glue into each hole and tap home a peg in each. Wipe away any surplus glue and leave to one side to dry. Complete both shoes in this way.

Fig. 69

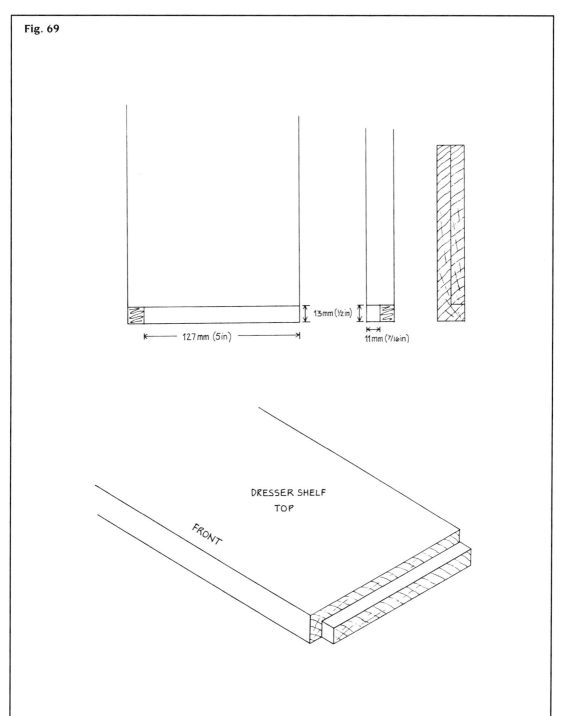

13mm (½in)

127mm (5in)

11mm (7/16in)

DRESSER SHELF
TOP

FRONT

Shelf end tenon

At the ends of both shelves a tenon has now to be formed to slot into the grooves on the rack sides. All the measurements needed to mark and cut them out are shown in fig. 69. (See also Mortise and Tenon Joints, *page* 134.)

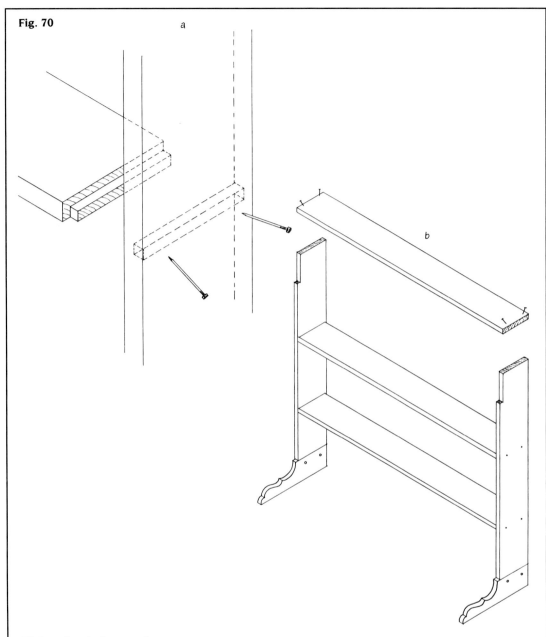

Fig. 70

a

b

Fixing the shelves and top

When the tenons fit securely into the grooves on the rack sides, the shelves can be fixed into place. Squeeze glue into the grooves on one side and push the tenons firmly into the grooves (fig. 70a); fix them using two 64mm (2½in) lost head nails in each joint. When one side has been completed, repeat the same procedure with the other end. Next, smear a layer of glue onto the top edge of the rack sides and lower the top board into position (fig. 70b). Fix using two 64mm (2½in) lost head nails in each end. Check that the rack is square, then place to one side to allow the glue to dry.

Fig. 71

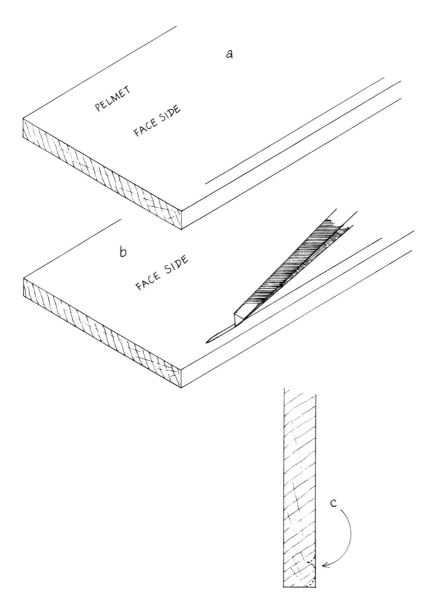

Pelmet moulding

To form the moulding on the lower front edge of the pelmet, set a gauge to 9.5mm (⅜in), and mark a line on the front of the pelmet to within 32mm (1¼in) of each end (fig. 71a). Then, using a saw file or a tool with a similarly-shaped end, run it up and down the gauge line until a V-shaped groove with a depth of about 5mm (³⁄₁₆in) has been obtained (fig. 71b). Finally, using a medium to coarse glasspaper first, followed by a fine one, round the two sharp edges at the top of the V-groove, and then the bottom front edge. This should now appear as a half round bead as shown in fig. 71c.

Fig. 72

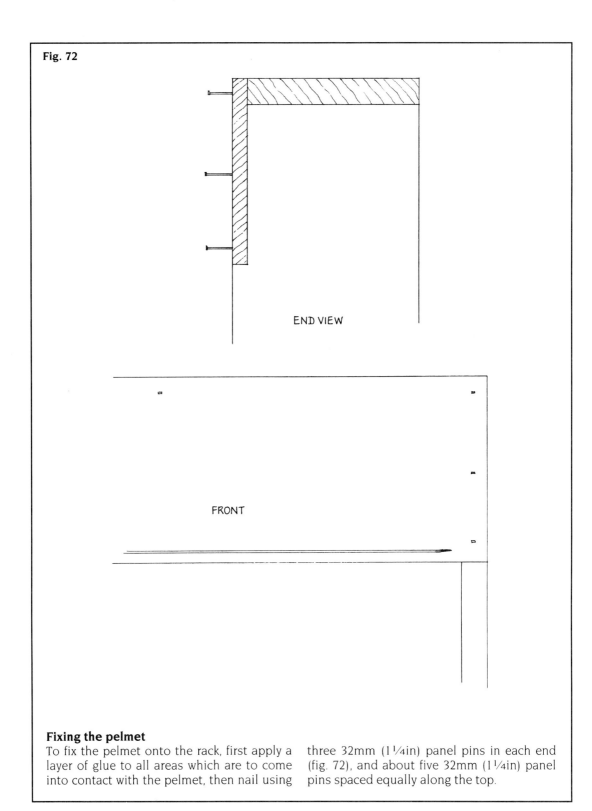

END VIEW

FRONT

Fixing the pelmet
To fix the pelmet onto the rack, first apply a layer of glue to all areas which are to come into contact with the pelmet, then nail using three 32mm (1¼in) panel pins in each end (fig. 72), and about five 32mm (1¼in) panel pins spaced equally along the top.

Fig. 73

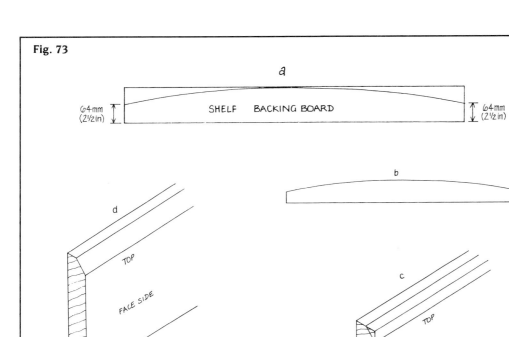

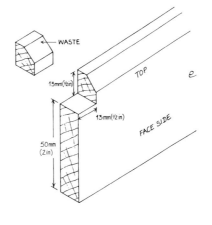

Shelf backing board

To form the curved shape on the top edge of the shelf backing, measure up 64mm (2½in) from the bottom, and mark each end of the board. Now draw a pencil line between these two lines, arching at the centre of the top to form a shallow curve as shown in fig. 73a. Secure the board in a vice and with a coping saw cut away the waste wood, leaving the desired shape (fig. 73b). This board can now be used to mark the two remaining backing boards.

When the three boards have been cut, sandpaper smooth the roughness made by the saw. Set a gauge to 6.4mm (¼in) and lightly mark one line on the top edge and one on the face as shown in fig. 73c. The area between the two lines should be planed away, forming the chamfer (fig. 73d). The final task is to remove the two top corners from all three of the backing boards. The size of the piece to be cut away is the same for all pieces – 13mm (½in) × 13mm (½in) – and it should be removed as shown in fig. 73e.

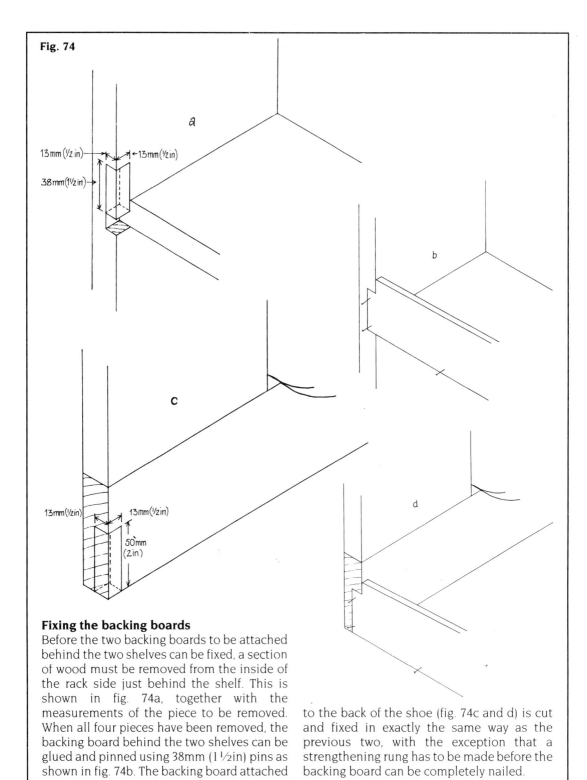

Fig. 74

13 mm (½ in) ←13 mm (½ in)

38 mm (1½ in)→

a

b

c

13 mm (½ in)   13 mm (½ in)

50 mm
(2 in)

d

Fixing the backing boards

Before the two backing boards to be attached behind the two shelves can be fixed, a section of wood must be removed from the inside of the rack side just behind the shelf. This is shown in fig. 74a, together with the measurements of the piece to be removed. When all four pieces have been removed, the backing board behind the two shelves can be glued and pinned using 38mm (1½in) pins as shown in fig. 74b. The backing board attached to the back of the shoe (fig. 74c and d) is cut and fixed in exactly the same way as the previous two, with the exception that a strengthening rung has to be made before the backing board can be completely nailed.

Fig. 75

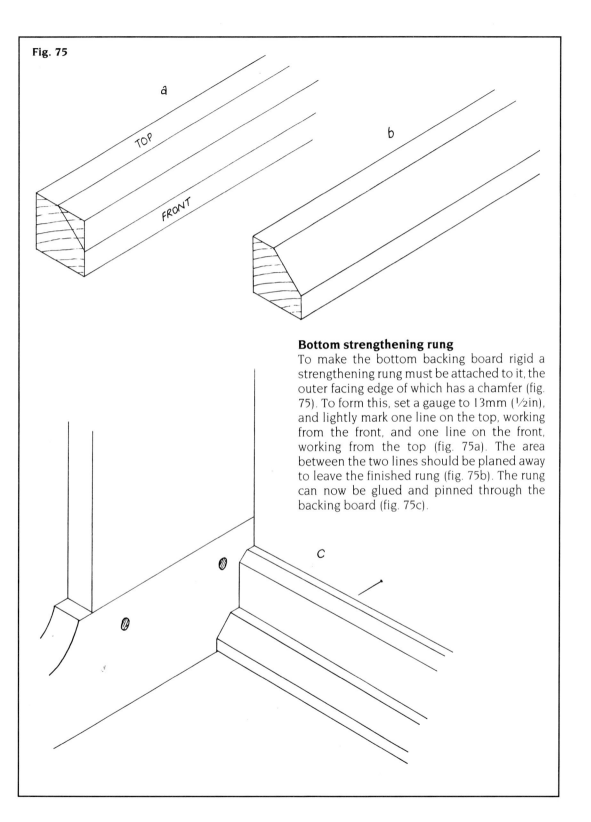

Bottom strengthening rung

To make the bottom backing board rigid a strengthening rung must be attached to it, the outer facing edge of which has a chamfer (fig. 75). To form this, set a gauge to 13mm (½in), and lightly mark one line on the top, working from the front, and one line on the front, working from the top (fig. 75a). The area between the two lines should be planed away to leave the finished rung (fig. 75b). The rung can now be glued and pinned through the backing board (fig. 75c).

Fig. 76

a

9.5mm 13mm
(3/8 in) (1/2 in)

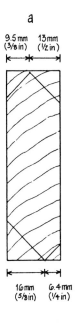

16mm 6.4mm
(5/8in) (1/4 in)

b

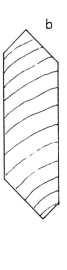

c

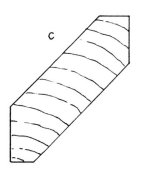

Making the top moulding

To make the shape for the top moulding, plane away all four corners at an angle of 45° to a depth shown in fig. 76a. When this has been done the timber should be of the shape shown in fig. 76b; the angle at which the moulding will be attached to the rack is shown in fig. 76c.

a

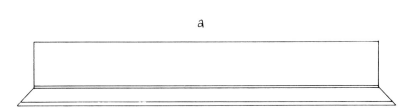

Cutting and fixing the moulding

The first piece of moulding to be cut and fixed is the front section. Hold the moulding onto the rack front at the angle at which it is to be fixed, and mark, mitre and cut the moulding as shown in fig. 77a. The edge to be attached to the rack front should be glued and the moulding pinned into position as shown in fig. 77b. Next, mark, mitre and cut the end pieces (fig. 77c) and glue and pin into position (fig. 77d).

All the pins in the dresser can now be punched just below the surface of the wood, so completing the construction. Finally, thoroughly sand the whole dresser, fill any nail or pin holes with a wax of a suitable colour, and finish using a stain, polish or wax of your choice.

Fig. 77

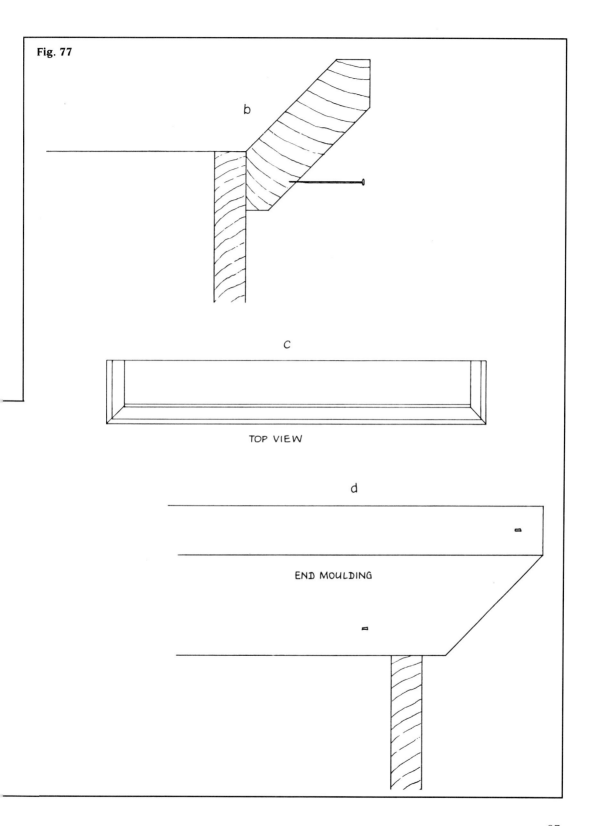

b

c

TOP VIEW

d

END MOULDING

7 Cupboard

Cupboards of a kind similar to this first appeared during the sixteenth and seventeenth centuries and were used in parlours and halls. These cupboards, sometimes used for storing food, were often called livery cupboards.

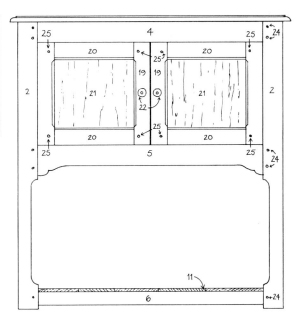

END

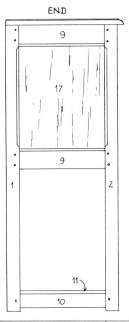

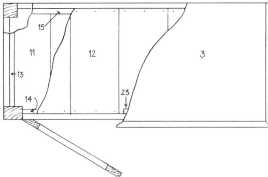

BACK

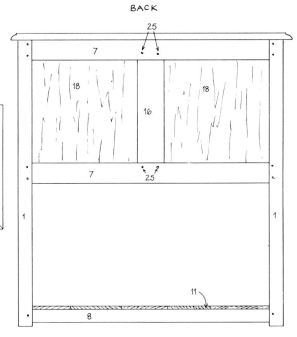

Cupboard showing part numbers.
Top size: 1066 × 457mm (42 × 18in)
Height: 1088mm (42⁷⁄₈in)
Timber: oak
Finish: oak stain and varnish

MATERIALS

Part no.	Part name	No. of pieces	Size	
1	Legs, back	2	1066 × 50 × 50mm	(42 × 2 × 2in)
2	Legs, front	2	1066 × 76 × 50mm	(42 × 3 × 2in)
3	Top	*	1066 × 457 × 22mm	(42 × 18 × 7/8in)
4	Top rail, front	1	940 × 76 × 22mm	(37 × 3 × 7/8in)
5	Mid rail, front	1	940 × 114 × 22mm	(37 × 4 1/2 × 7/8in)
6	Bottom rail, front	1	940 × 50 × 22mm	(37 × 2 × 7/8in)
7	Top and middle rails, back	2	991 × 76 × 22mm	(39 × 3 × 7/8in)
8	Bottom rail, back	1	991 × 50 × 22mm	(39 × 2 × 7/8in)
9	End rails, top and middle	4	381 × 76 × 22mm	(15 × 3 × 7/8in)
10	End rails, bottom	2	381 × 50 × 22mm	(15 × 2 × 7/8in)
11	Pot board	*	1015 × 432 × 13mm	(40 × 17 × 1/2in)
12	Cupboard bottom	*	972 × 387 × 13mm	(38 1/4 × 15 1/4 × 1/2in)
13	Cupboard bottom support battens, end	2	330 × 38 × 22mm	(13 × 1 1/2 × 7/8in)
14	Cupboard bottom support batten, front	1	863 × 38 × 22mm	(34 × 1 1/2 × 7/8in)
15	Cupboard bottom support batten, back	1	914 × 34 × 22mm	(36 × 1 1/2 × 7/8in)
16	Back middle upright	1	432 × 101 × 22mm	(17 × 4 × 7/8in)
17	End panels	2	394 × 343 × 13mm	(15 1/2 × 13 1/2 × 1/2in)
18	Back panels	2	394 × 419 × 13mm	(15 1/2 × 16 1/2 × 1/2in)
19	Door side rails	4	381 × 64 × 22mm	(15 × 2 1/2 × 7/8in)
20	Door top and bottom rails	4	381 × 64 × 22mm	(15 × 2 1/2 × 7/8in)
21	Door panels	2	317 × 267 × 13mm	(12 1/2 × 10 1/2 × 1/2in)
22	Door knobs (if required)	2	76 × 38 × 38mm	(3 × 1 1/2 × 1 1/2in)
23	Door stop block	1	89 × 38 × 13mm	(3 1/2 × 1 1/2 × 1/2in)
24	Dowel pegs	40	32 × 6.4mm	(1 1/4 × 1/4in)
25	Dowel pegs	12	25 × 6.4mm	(1 × 1/4in)

Wood glue

2 pairs of hinges, 76mm (3in), iron or brass, and screws to fix

22 no. 10 steel countersunk screws, 38mm (1 1/2in)

2 no. 8 steel countersunk screws, 25mm (1in)

Approximately 45 nails, 38mm (1 1/2in), for fixing pot board and cupboard bottom

* number depends on board widths available

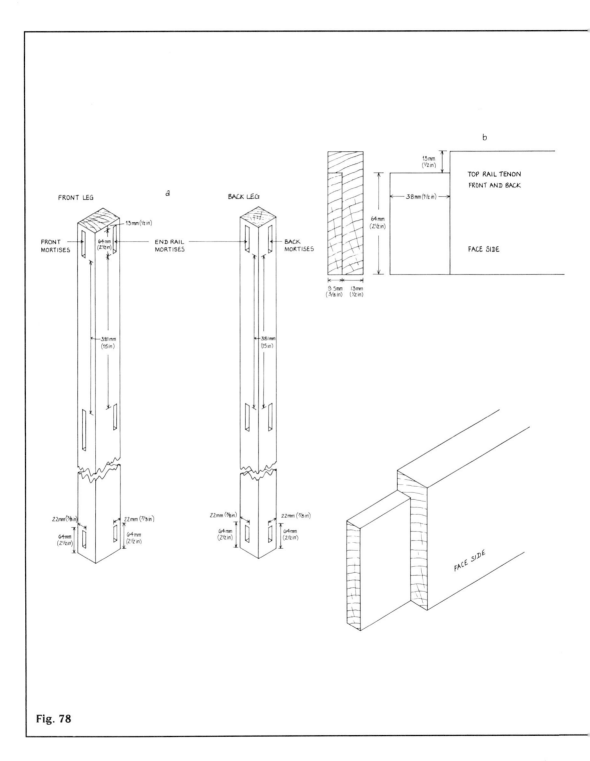

FRONT LEG   a   BACK LEG

13mm (½in)

FRONT MORTISES   64mm (2½in)

END RAIL MORTISES

BACK MORTISES

b

13mm (½in)

TOP RAIL TENON FRONT AND BACK

38mm (1½in)

64mm (2½in)

FACE SIDE

9.5mm (3/8in)   13mm (½in)

381mm (15in)

381mm (15in)

22mm (7/8in)   22mm (7/8in)

64mm (2½in)   64mm (2½in)

22mm (7/8in)   22mm (7/8in)

64mm (2½in)   64mm (2½in)

FACE SIDE

Fig. 78

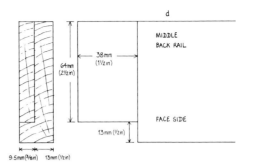

c

MIDDLE RAIL FRONT

FACE SIDE

38mm (1½in)

101mm (4in)

13mm (½in)

9.5mm (3/8in) 13mm (½in)

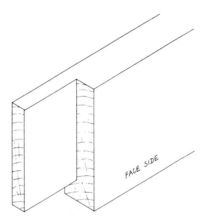

d

MIDDLE BACK RAIL

FACE SIDE

38mm (1½in)

64mm (2½in)

13mm (½in)

9.5mm(3/8in) 13mm (½in)

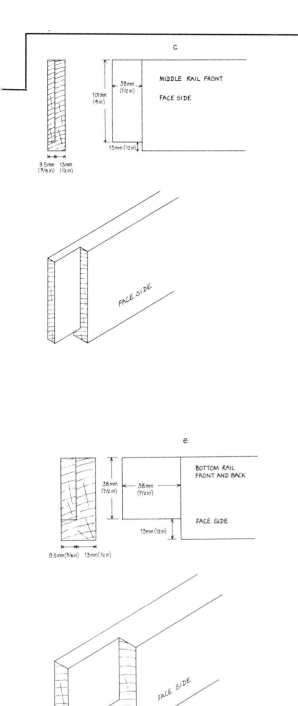

FACE SIDE

e

BOTTOM RAIL FRONT AND BACK

FACE SIDE

38mm (1½in)

38mm (1½in)

13mm (½in)

9.5mm(3/8in) 13mm (½in)

FACE SIDE

FACE SIDE

Joints

The first step in constructing the cupboard is to mark and cut all mortise and tenon joints in the cupboard frame. Fig. 78a shows a front leg and a back leg together with all the necessary measurements required to mark and cut the mortises. Fig. 78b shows the size of the tenons to be cut on the top rail, front and back, fig. 78c the tenon for the front mid rail, and fig. 78d the tenon for the back mid rail. The bottom rails, front and back, are shown in fig. 78e.

101

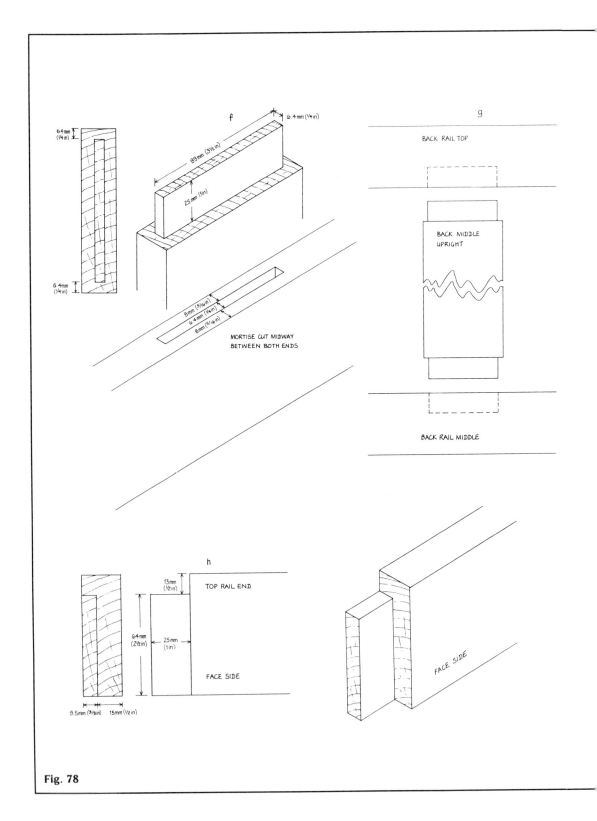

f

6.4mm (¼ in)

89mm (3½ in)

25mm (1in)

6.4 mm
(¼ in)

6.4mm
(¼ in)

8mm (5/16 in)
6.4mm (¼ in)
8mm (5/16 in)

MORTISE CUT MIDWAY
BETWEEN BOTH ENDS

g

BACK RAIL TOP

BACK MIDDLE
UPRIGHT

BACK RAIL MIDDLE

h

13mm
(½ in)

TOP RAIL END

64mm
(2½ in)

25mm
(1in)

FACE SIDE

9.5mm (3/8in)   13mm (½ in)

FACE SIDE

Fig. 78

102

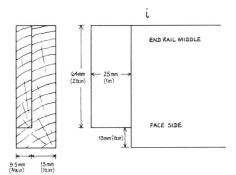

i

END RAIL MIDDLE

64mm (2½in)   25mm (1in)

FACE SIDE

13mm (½in)

9.5mm (3/8in)   13mm (½in)

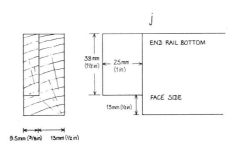

j

END RAIL BOTTOM

38mm (1½in)   25mm (1in)

FACE SIDE

13mm (½in)

9.5mm (3/8in)   13mm (½in)

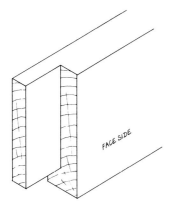

FACE SIDE

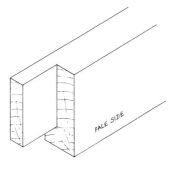

FACE SIDE

Both the mortise and tenon joints that secure the back upright into position are shown in fig. 78f and g, together with all the measurements required. The tenons on both top end rails are shown in fig. 78h, the tenons for the middle end rails in fig. 78i, and the tenons on the bottom end rails are shown in fig. 78j. When all these joints have been cut, run through a trial assembly to make sure all joints fit, then dismantle and proceed to the next stage.

Fig. 79

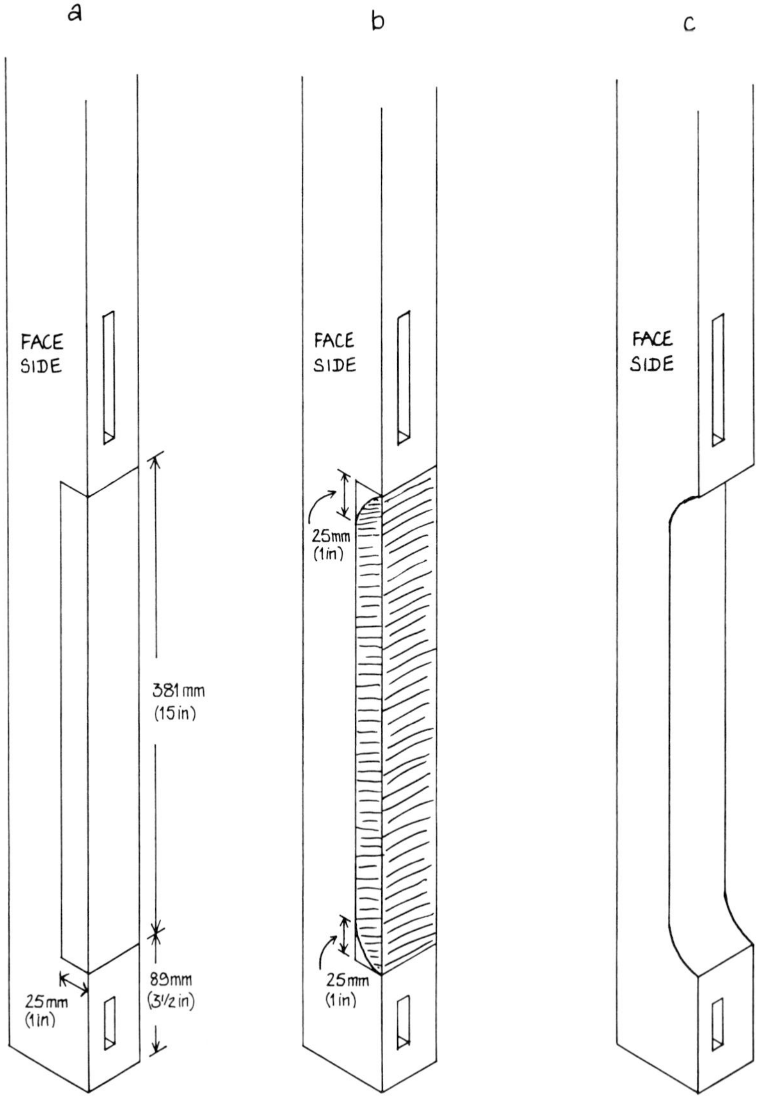

a   b   c

FACE SIDE

FACE SIDE

FACE SIDE

381 mm
(15 in)

25 mm
(1 in)

25 mm
(1 in)

89 mm
(3½ in)

25 mm
(1 in)

Shaping the front legs

To bring the front legs into proportion with the back legs a shaped section has been created on the inside edges. Mark both front legs as shown in fig. 79a and b, then, with a coping saw, cut away the area shaded. The finished shape will then appear as shown in fig. 79c. Any roughness made by the saw can be papered away using a medium to coarse sandpaper, finishing off with a fine one.

Fig. 80

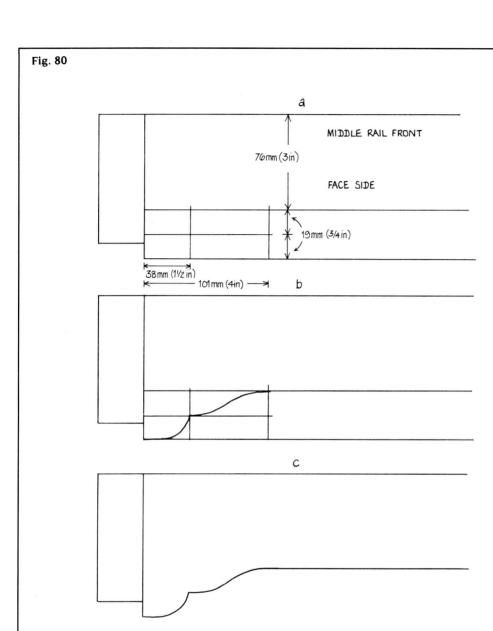

a

MIDDLE RAIL FRONT

76mm (3in)

FACE SIDE

19mm (3/4 in)

38mm (1½ in)

101mm (4in)

b

c

Shaping on mid front rail

To form the shaping at each end of the middle front rail, mark out each end using the measurements shown in fig. 80a. Next, using the guide lines, draw in the shape shown in fig. 80b. The whole lower section can now be cut away with a coping saw, leaving the finished shape as shown in fig. 80c.

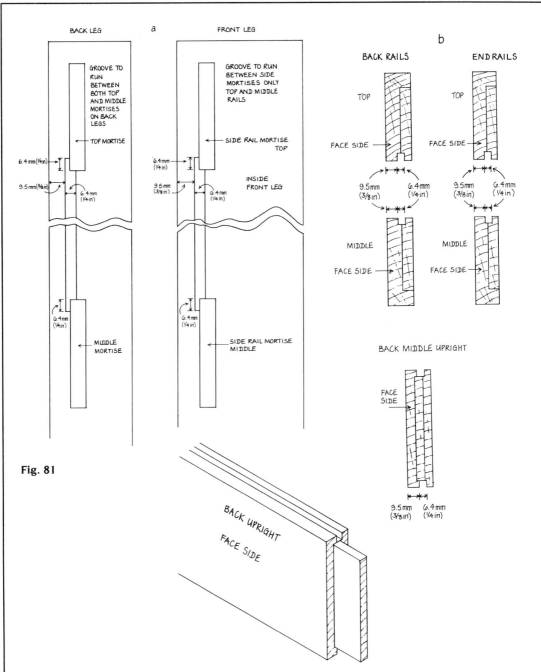

Fig. 81

Grooves to house panels

In order to secure the end and back panels into the frame, grooves have to be formed. These are all 6.4 × 6.4mm (¼ × ¼in), and are 9.5mm (⅜in) in from the face side. The location of the grooves set in the leg section can be seen in fig. 81a, together with all the necessary details for cutting them. The grooves in the rails are shown in fig. 81b. (See also Mouldings, *page* 127.)

Fig. 82

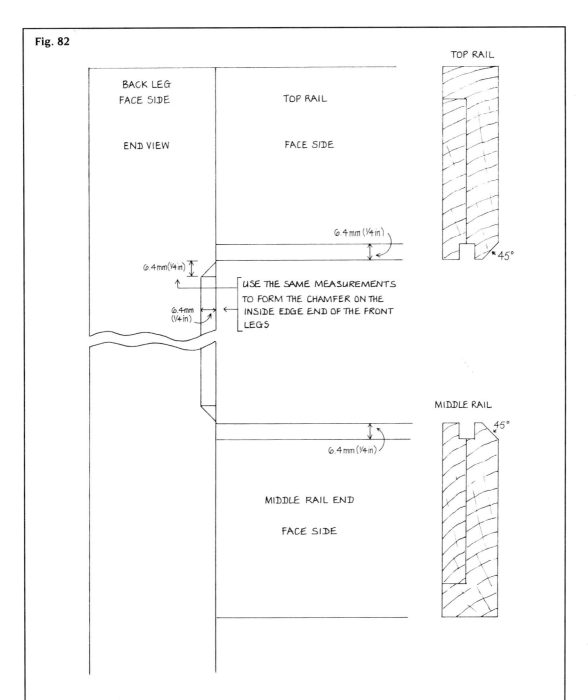

TOP RAIL

BACK LEG
FACE SIDE

TOP RAIL

END VIEW

FACE SIDE

6.4 mm (¼ in)

6.4mm(¼in)

45°

6.4mm
(¼in)

USE THE SAME MEASUREMENTS
TO FORM THE CHAMFER ON THE
INSIDE EDGE END OF THE FRONT
LEGS

MIDDLE RAIL

45°

6.4 mm (¼ in)

MIDDLE RAIL END

FACE SIDE

Forming the chamfers

To remove the sharp edges and generally improve the overall appearance, chamfers have been formed to surround the end panels. The chamfer on the upper end section of the front and back legs runs between the top and middle rails. On the top and middle end rails it runs the full length. Full details can be seen in fig. 82. (See also Mouldings, *page* 127.)

Fig. 83

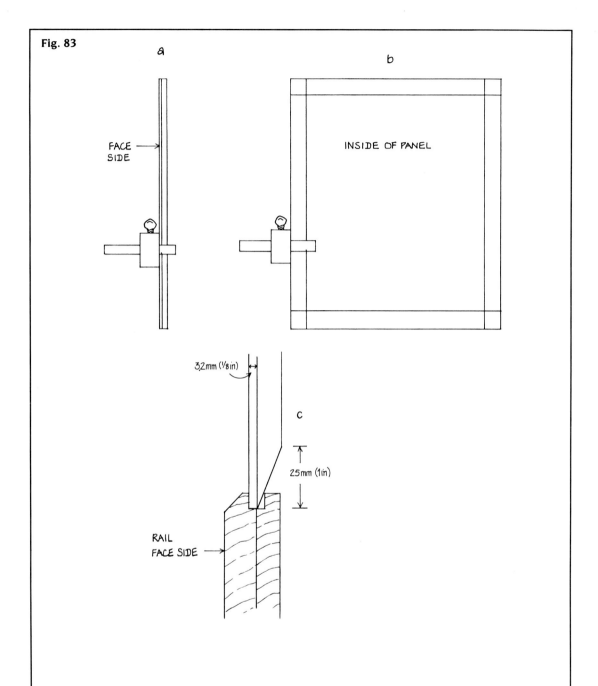

a

FACE
SIDE →

b

INSIDE OF PANEL

32mm (⅛in)

c

25mm (1in)

RAIL
FACE SIDE →

Shaping the panels

To allow the end and back panels to slot into the grooves, a large chamfer has to be made on the inside of all four panels. Set a gauge to 3.2mm (⅛in) and, working from the face side, gauge a line around all four edges of each panel (fig. 83a). Reset the gauge to 25mm (1in) and, working from the edge, gauge a line around the inside of each panel (fig. 83b). The area between the two lines can now be planed away, allowing the panels to drop into the grooves (fig. 83c).

Fig. 84

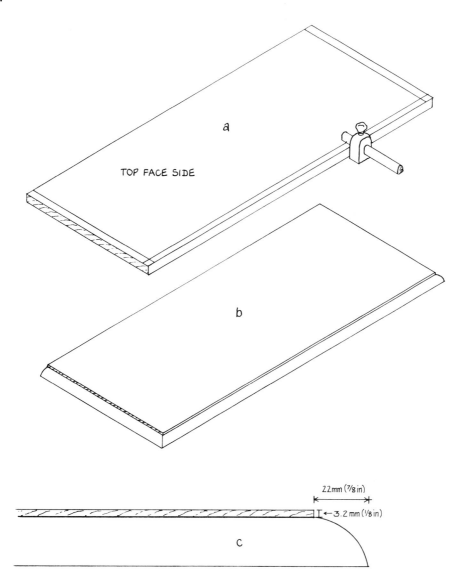

a

TOP FACE SIDE

b

22mm (⅞ in)

|← 3.2 mm (⅛ in)

c

Forming the top moulding

To form the moulding on the cupboard top, set a gauge to 22mm (⅞in) and mark a line on the top, working the gauge along the front and both ends (fig. 84a). To complete the moulding as shown in fig. 84b and c, see Mouldings, *page* 127.

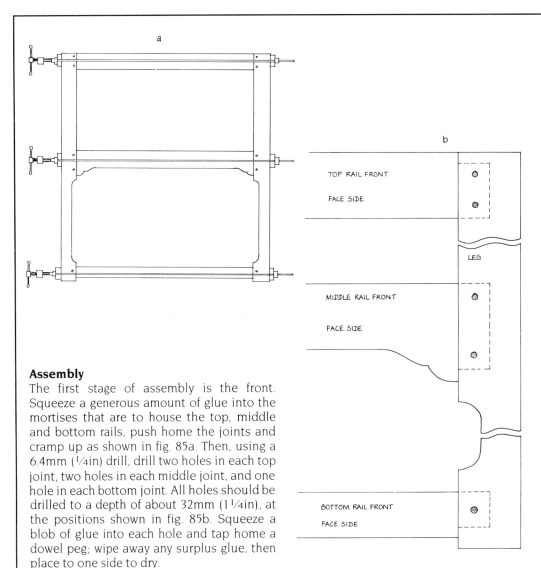

a

b

TOP RAIL FRONT

FACE SIDE

LEG

MIDDLE RAIL FRONT

FACE SIDE

BOTTOM RAIL FRONT

FACE SIDE

Assembly

The first stage of assembly is the front. Squeeze a generous amount of glue into the mortises that are to house the top, middle and bottom rails, push home the joints and cramp up as shown in fig. 85a. Then, using a 6.4mm ($\frac{1}{4}$in) drill, drill two holes in each top joint, two holes in each middle joint, and one hole in each bottom joint. All holes should be drilled to a depth of about 32mm (1$\frac{1}{4}$in), at the positions shown in fig. 85b. Squeeze a blob of glue into each hole and tap home a dowel peg; wipe away any surplus glue, then place to one side to dry.

To glue up the back section, first run glue into the mortises that are to house the back upright, push it into position between the top and middle back rails and cramp up. In each joint drill two 6.4mm ($\frac{1}{4}$in) holes through the frame at the positions shown in fig. 85c. Squeeze a blob of glue into each hole and tap home a 22mm ($\frac{7}{8}$in) long dowel peg in each. Next, run glue into the mortises that are to house the top, middle and bottom rails, slide the two back panels into position between the top and middle rails, and assemble, using the same procedure as for gluing up the front.

When the front and back sections are perfectly dry, the end pieces can be attached. Squeeze a generous amount of glue into all the remaining mortises and push home the top, middle and bottom rails into the back section. Slide in the two end panels and push on the front section. The whole frame can now be cramped, drilled and pegged using the same method as for gluing up the front. The positions at which the pegs are to be placed in each joint are shown in fig. 85d, and the completed end section is shown in fig. 85e.

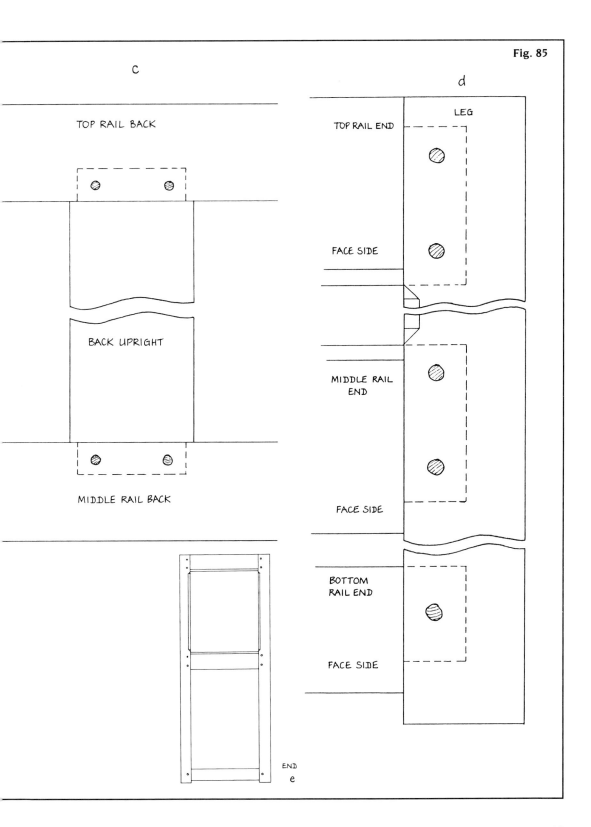

Fig. 85

c

TOP RAIL BACK

d

TOP RAIL END

LEG

FACE SIDE

BACK UPRIGHT

MIDDLE RAIL
END

MIDDLE RAIL BACK

FACE SIDE

BOTTOM
RAIL END

FACE SIDE

END

e

Fig. 86

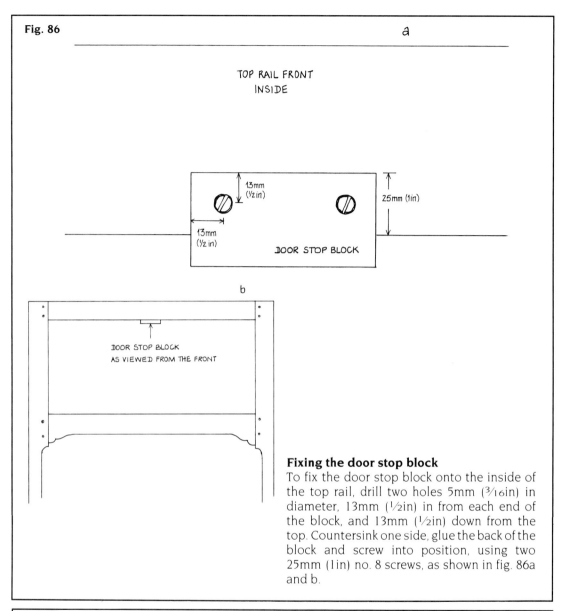

a

TOP RAIL FRONT
INSIDE

13mm
(½in)

25mm (1in)

13mm
(½in)

DOOR STOP BLOCK

b

DOOR STOP BLOCK
AS VIEWED FROM THE FRONT

Fixing the door stop block

To fix the door stop block onto the inside of the top rail, drill two holes 5mm (³⁄₁₆in) in diameter, 13mm (½in) in from each end of the block, and 13mm (½in) down from the top. Countersink one side, glue the back of the block and screw into position, using two 25mm (1in) no. 8 screws, as shown in fig. 86a and b.

Fig. 87

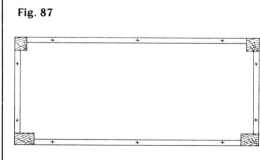

Fixing the top

To fix the cupboard top onto the frame, drill ten holes at the positions shown in fig. 87. The angle of the hole to be drilled and further fixing instructions are shown in fig. 16b, c and d. The cupboard top should be screwed into position using 38mm (1½in) no. 8 steel countersunk screws, and should overhang the front and each end by 25mm (1in).

Fig. 88

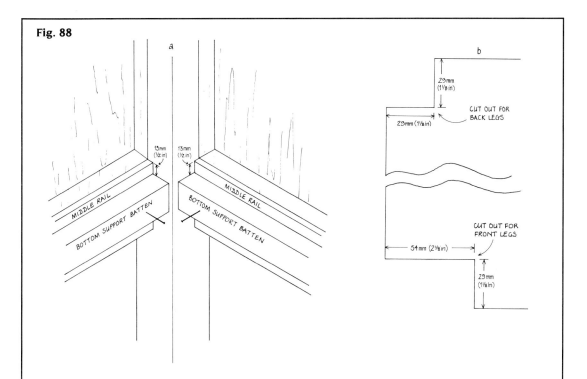

Cupboard bottom support battens

Lay the four cupboard support battens flat on the bench and in each of the two long ones tap in five 38mm (1½in) pins or nails until the points just appear through the wood; tap in three in the two end battens. Smear a layer of glue along the length of each batten and fix it 13mm (½in) below the middle rail as shown in fig. 88.

Fixing the cupboard bottom

As the cupboard bottom is made up by butting a number of boards together, the two end boards are best cut and fixed first since these notch around the leg section. Select the two boards that are to be used as end boards and cut the corners away (fig. 88b and c). The remainder of the boards can now be cut, fitted and pinned into position (fig. 88d).

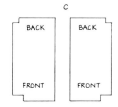

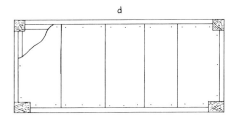

Pot board

The procedure for fixing the pot board is the same as on the dresser, and the details in fig. 58 can once again be used.

Doors

Fig. 89

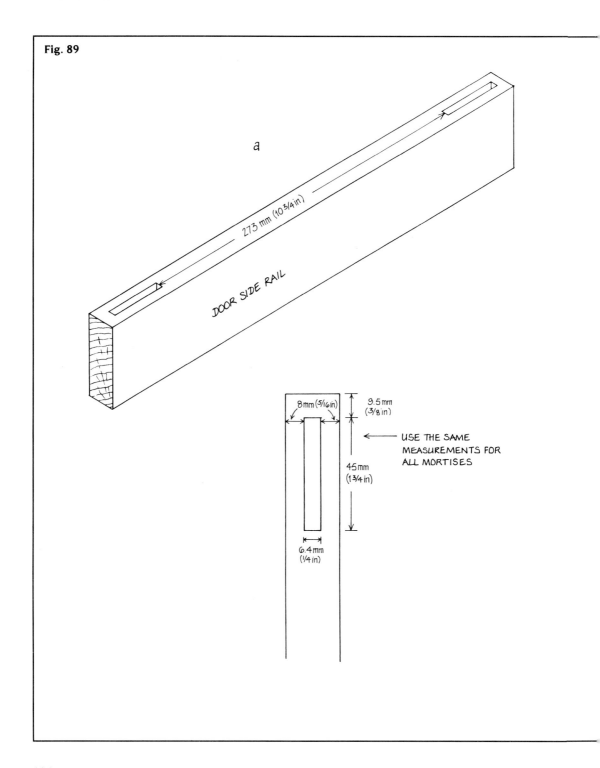

a

273 mm (10 3/4 in)

DOOR SIDE RAIL

8 mm (5/16 in)

9.5 mm (3/8 in)

← USE THE SAME MEASUREMENTS FOR ALL MORTISES

45 mm (1 3/4 in)

6.4 mm (1/4 in)

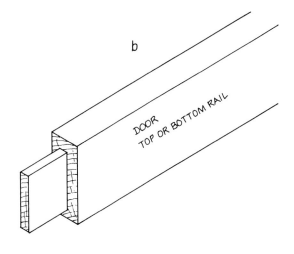

b

DOOR
TOP OR BOTTOM RAIL

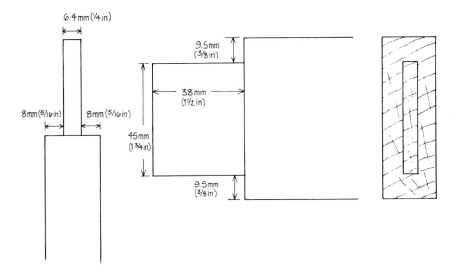

6.4mm (¼ in)

9.5mm
(⅜ in)

38mm
(1½ in)

8mm (5/16 in)   8mm (5/16 in)

45mm
(1¾ in)

9.5mm
(⅜ in)

Mortise and tenon joints

The first step towards making the doors is to mark and cut the mortise and tenon joints. The size and location of the mortises cut into the side rails are shown in fig. 89a and the tenons on the top and bottom rails are shown in fig. 89b, together with all the measurements required to cut them. (See also Mortise and Tenon Joints, *page* 134.)

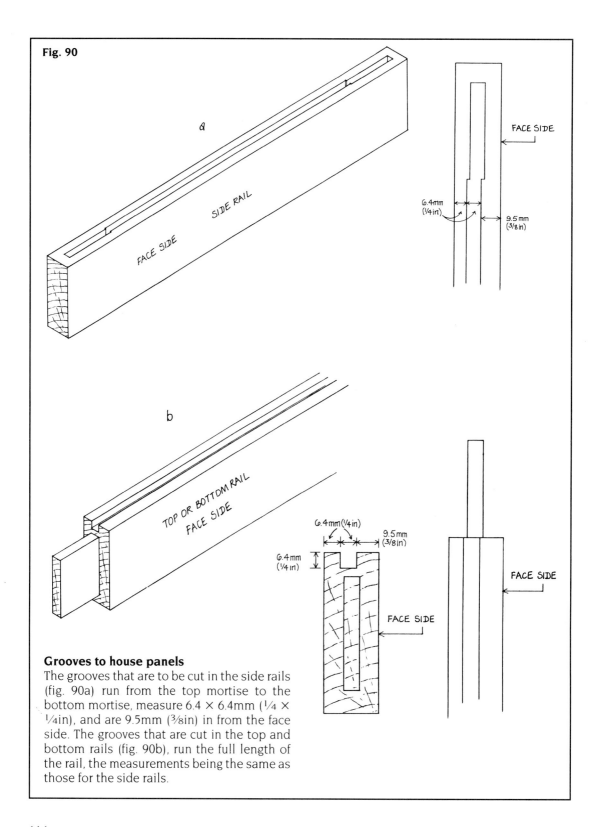

Fig. 90

a

SIDE RAIL

FACE SIDE

FACE SIDE

6.4mm (¼in)

9.5mm (³⁄₈in)

b

TOP OR BOTTOM RAIL
FACE SIDE

6.4mm (¼in)

9.5mm (³⁄₈in)

6.4mm (¼in)

FACE SIDE

FACE SIDE

Grooves to house panels

The grooves that are to be cut in the side rails (fig. 90a) run from the top mortise to the bottom mortise, measure 6.4 × 6.4mm (¼ × ¼in), and are 9.5mm (³⁄₈in) in from the face side. The grooves that are cut in the top and bottom rails (fig. 90b), run the full length of the rail, the measurements being the same as those for the side rails.

Fig. 91

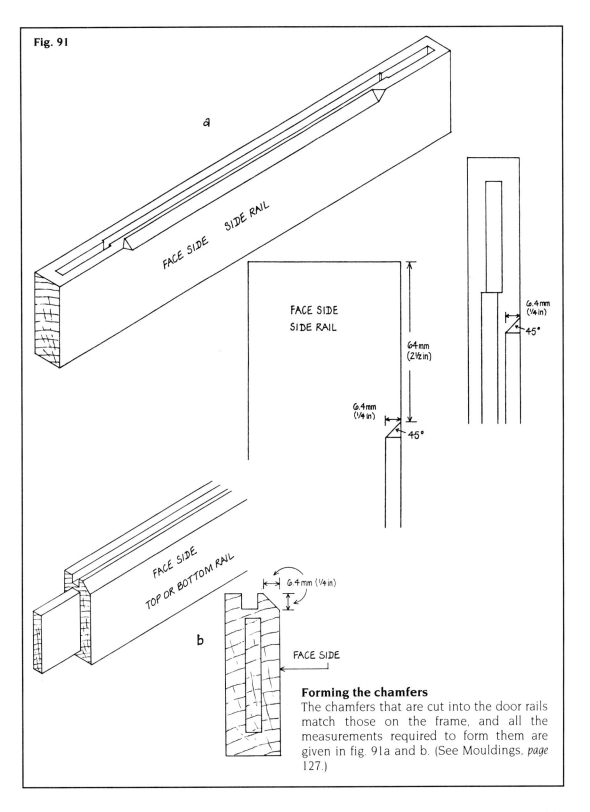

a

FACE SIDE   SIDE RAIL

FACE SIDE
SIDE RAIL

64mm
(2½in)

6.4mm
(¼in)

45°

6.4mm
(¼in)

45°

FACE SIDE
TOP OR BOTTOM RAIL

b

6.4mm (¼in)

FACE SIDE

Forming the chamfers

The chamfers that are cut into the door rails match those on the frame, and all the measurements required to form them are given in fig. 91a and b. (See Mouldings, *page* 127.)

117

Shaping the panels

The door panels have now to be chamfered on the inside to allow them to slot into the grooves. To do this, follow the instructions in fig. 83 as the measurements and procedure are the same.

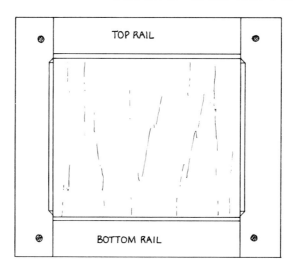

Fig. 92

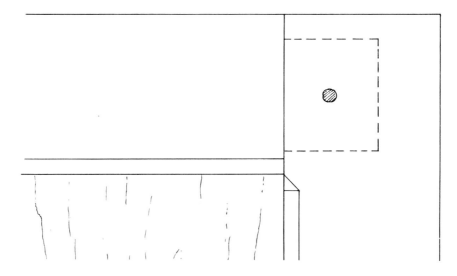

Door assembly

To assemble the doors, squeeze a generous amount of glue into each mortise, push home the top and bottom rail tenons into one side rail, slide in the panel and then push home the other side rail. Cramp up and then, using a 6.4mm (¼in) bit, drill one hole through each joint at the location shown in fig. 92. Squeeze a blob of glue in each hole and tap in a peg. Wipe away any surplus glue and place to one side to dry.

Fig. 93

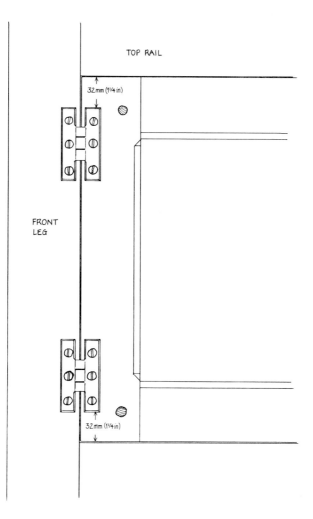

TOP RAIL

32 mm (1¼ in)

FRONT
LEG

32 mm (1¼ in)

Fixing the hinges

The hinges used on this cupboard are brass H hinges, though any surface fixing hinge would be suitable. Fig. 93 shows the position in which the hinges are fitted; as they are of a surface-fixing type, little skill is needed to fix them. Simply lay them onto the frame, start a hole for the screws with a bradawl and screw on.

Handles

Turned wooden knobs have been fitted to the cupboard illustrated, but the choice of handle rests with the individual's personal taste. If a wooden knob is preferred, the one used on this piece can be found, together with the necessary measurements, on *page* 139.

Finally, sandpaper the completed piece to a finish, then apply the polish or wax of your choice.

⑧ Joint Stool

The joint stool first appeared around the sixteenth century when it took over from the trestle or boarded stool. It was normally constructed of oak but can also be found in yew and elm.

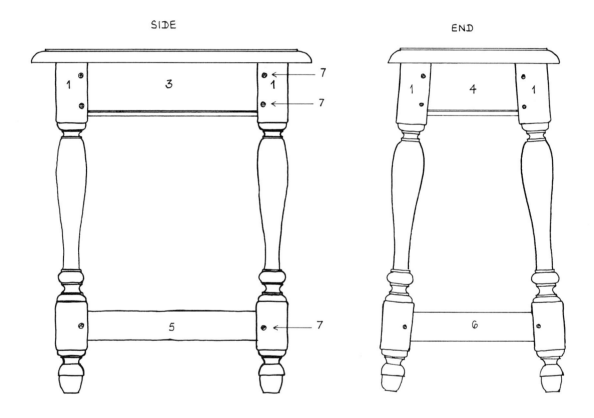

SIDE   END

Joint stool showing part numbers.
Top size: 457 × 280mm (18 × 11in)
Height: 543mm (21³⁄₈in)
Timber: yew
Finish: waxed

PLAN

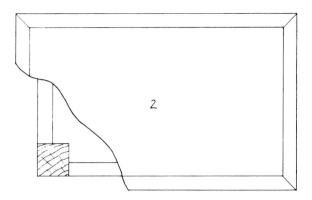

MATERIALS

Part no.	Part name	No. of pieces	Size	
1*	Legs	4	559 × 48 × 48mm	(22 × 1⅞ × 1⅞in)
2	Top	1	457 × 280 × 22mm	(18 × 11 × ⅞in)
3	Top rails, side	2	330 × 83 × 22mm	(13 × 3¼ × ⅞in)
4	Top rails, end	2	203 × 83 × 22mm	(8 × 3¼ × ⅞in)
5	Bottom rails, side	2	330 × 45 × 22mm	(13 × 1¾ × ⅞in)
6	Bottom rails, end	2	254 × 45 × 22mm	(10 × 1¾ × ⅞in)
7	Dowel pegs	24	32 × 6.4mm	(1¼ × ¼in)

Wood glue
4 no. 8 steel countersunk screws, 38mm (1½in)

* An extra 38mm (1½in) has been added to the length of the legs to allow for wastage when turned. The finished length will therefore be 521mm (20½in).

CONSTRUCTION

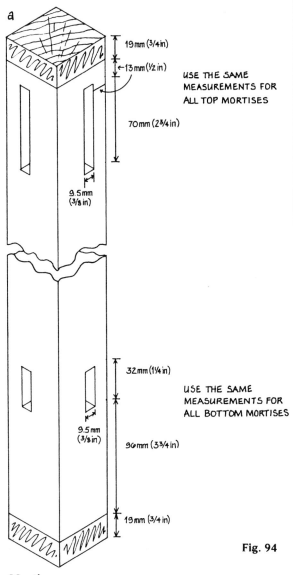

a

19mm (3/4 in)

←13mm (1/2 in)

USE THE SAME
MEASUREMENTS FOR
ALL TOP MORTISES

70mm (2¾ in)

9.5mm
(3/8 in)

32mm (1¼ in)

USE THE SAME
MEASUREMENTS FOR
ALL BOTTOM MORTISES

9.5mm
(3/8 in)

96mm (3¾ in)

19mm (3/4 in)

Fig. 94

Mortises

The first step in constructing the joint stool is to mark and cut the mortise and tenon joints. The mortises are shown in fig. 94a, together with all the necessary measurements. The shaded area at each end of the leg, shown also in fig. 94a, is waste wood and will be removed when the leg is turned in the lathe at a later stage. (See also Mortise and Tenon Joints, *page 134.*)

Tenons

The tenons on the top side rails are shown in fig. 94b, together with all the necessary measurements required to mark and cut them, and the tenons on the bottom side rails are shown in fig. 94c. Although this stool is square from the side, the ends are splayed to give extra stability. To obtain this shape the shoulders of the tenons must be cut at an angle of 85° (fig. 94d), though the tenons themselves are the same size as those on the side rails.

Fig. 94

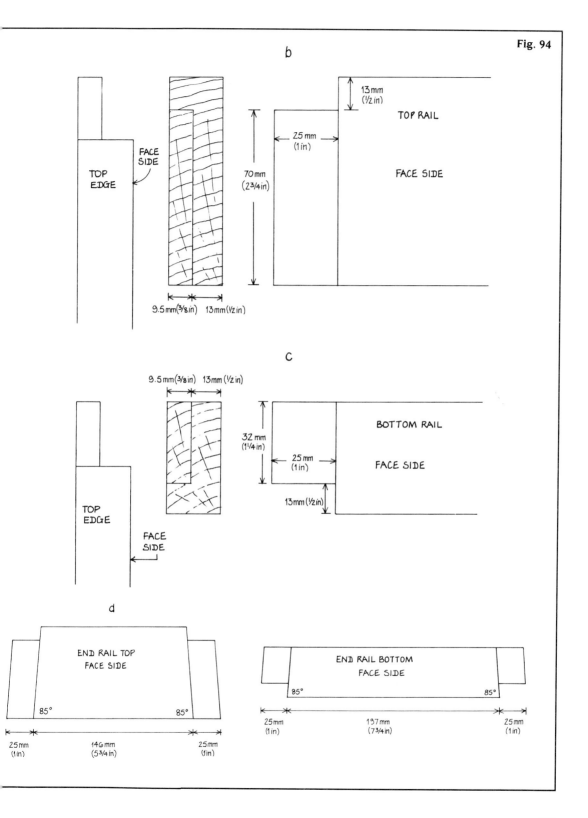

b

FACE SIDE

TOP EDGE

70 mm (2³/₄ in)

9.5 mm (³/₈ in)   13 mm (½ in)

13 mm (½ in)

TOP RAIL

25 mm (1 in)

FACE SIDE

c

9.5 mm (³/₈ in)   13 mm (½ in)

TOP EDGE

FACE SIDE

32 mm (1¹/₄ in)

25 mm (1 in)

13 mm (½ in)

BOTTOM RAIL

FACE SIDE

d

END RAIL TOP
FACE SIDE

85°   85°

25 mm (1 in)   146 mm (5³/₄ in)   25 mm (1 in)

END RAIL BOTTOM
FACE SIDE

85°   85°

25 mm (1 in)   197 mm (7³/₄ in)   25 mm (1 in)

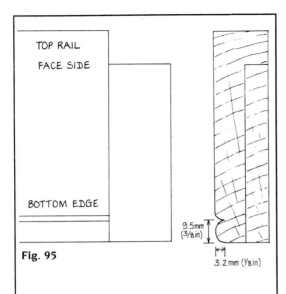

TOP RAIL

FACE SIDE

BOTTOM EDGE

9.5mm
(3/8 in)

3.2 mm (1/8 in)

Fig. 95

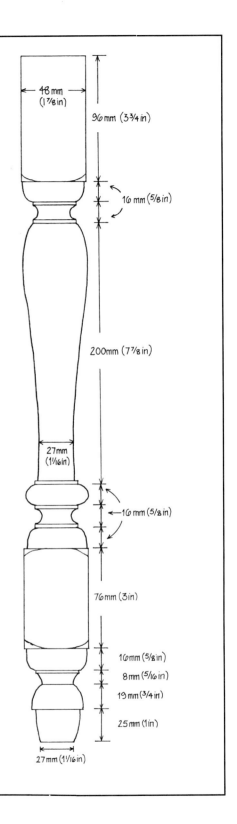

48 mm
(1 7/8 in)

96 mm (3 3/4 in)

16 mm (5/8 in)

200mm (7 7/8 in)

27mm
(1 1/16 in)

16 mm (5/8 in)

76mm (3in)

16mm (5/8 in)

8 mm (5/16 in)

19 mm (3/4 in)

25 mm (1 in)

27mm (1 1/16 in)

Fig. 96

Top rail moulding
On the bottom front corner of all the top rails a very simple moulding has been formed. Fig. 95 shows the moulding together with all the necessary measurements. In all cases the moulding runs the full length of the rail, and by referring back to fig. 71 the technique of forming it can be seen.

Turning the legs
The last job prior to assembly is to turn the legs. In fig. 96 a leg has been illustrated, together with the basic measurements. There is no need to worry if the leg does not turn out exactly the same as the drawing or, in fact, if all four legs are not identical. A hand-produced piece of furniture can have slight variations – that is what makes it individual.

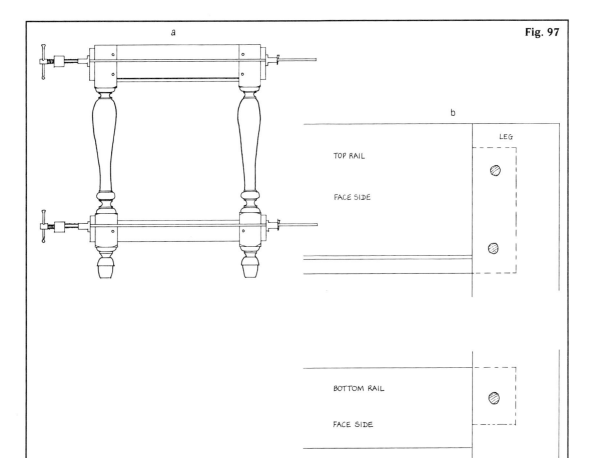

a

Fig. 97

b

LEG

TOP RAIL

FACE SIDE

BOTTOM RAIL

FACE SIDE

Assembly

Squeeze glue into the two mortises in each leg that are to take the side rails, push the rails into position and cramp up as shown in fig. 97a. Drill two 6.4mm (¼in) holes in each of the top joints and one 6.4mm (¼in) hole in each of the bottom ones. Each hole should be drilled to a depth of about 32mm (1¼in), and at the approximate positions shown in fig. 97b. Drop a blob of glue into each hole and tap home one of the pegs in each. Wipe away any surplus glue and place both side frames to one side to dry before attempting to glue on the ends. When the side frames are dry, squeeze glue into the remaining mortises, push the rails into their positions and cramp up (fig. 97c). The holes for the dowel pegs should be drilled using the same positions as for the side rails.

c

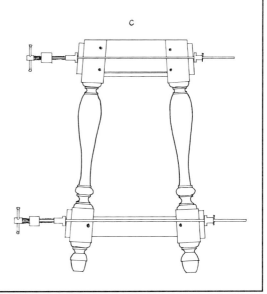

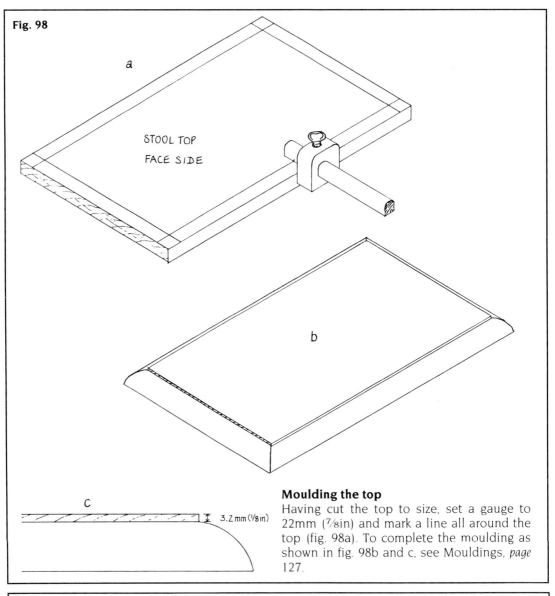

Fig. 98

a

STOOL TOP

FACE SIDE

b

c

3.2 mm (⅛ in)

Moulding the top

Having cut the top to size, set a gauge to 22mm (⅞in) and mark a line all around the top (fig. 98a). To complete the moulding as shown in fig. 98b and c, see Mouldings, *page 127*.

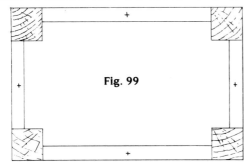

Fig. 99

Fixing the top

To fix the top onto the frame, drill four holes at the positions shown in fig. 99. The angle of the holes can be seen by referring back to fig. 16 b c and d. When the holes have been drilled, lay the stool top upside down on the bench, centralize the frame on it and screw into position.

Sandpaper the stool to a finish and apply the polish or wax of your choice.

⑨ Mouldings

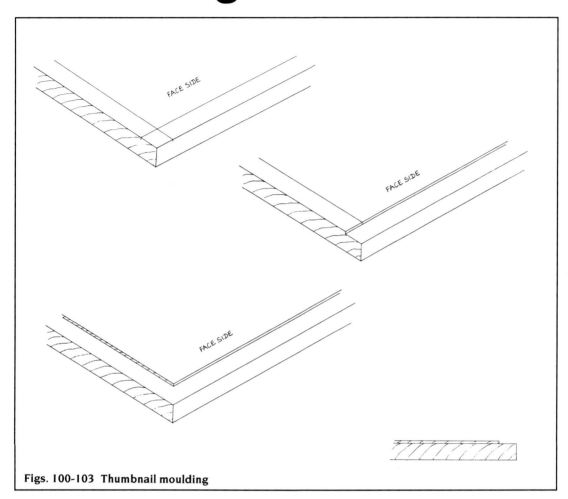

Figs. 100-103 Thumbnail moulding

There are two mouldings on the furniture in this book. The first is the thumbnail moulding, used on tops and drawer front edges. It is quite simple to form and gives a very pleasing finish. The other moulding is simply a chamfer and has been formed not only to improve the overall appearance of the piece, but also to remove the sharp edges in places that would normally be liable to damage.

Thumbnail moulding

Having prepared your work to the stage shown in fig. 100, take a Stanley knife or similar sharp knife and carefully cut down into the gauge lines. If the piece is a top the depth of cut should be about 3.2mm (⅛in). In the case of a drawer front, the depth should be about half that – 1.5mm (¹⁄₁₆in). Next, using a rebate plane and working first with the grain, remove the section of wood shown in fig. 101, the depth being determined by whether it is a drawer front or top. The cross-grain section of waste can now be removed with a rebate plane (figs. 102 and 103). The purpose of removing the end-grain waste last is to avoid the unnecessary splitting at the corners, which would almost certainly occur.

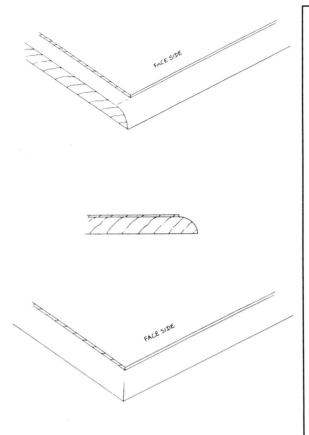

Figs. 104-106 Thumbnail moulding

Finally, using a plane, round the edges as shown in figs. 104 and 105; rounding the end grain is again left until last to avoid splitting (fig. 106). A medium and then fine sandpapering should now be given to the moulding until a satisfactory finish has been obtained.

Chamfer

The chamfer shown in fig. 107 is formed by running a plane along the edge of the timber at an angle of 45°. However, when it is necessary to stop the chamfer short of the end as shown in fig. 108, the following technique must be applied. Using a sharp chisel about 13mm (½in) wide, position it at an angle of 45° (fig. 109), with a 45° backward lean (fig. 110), at a point about 13mm (½in) from the 45° line (fig. 110). Tap the chisel firmly into the wood, remove and repeat, taking two or three cuts to reach the 45° angle line (fig. 111). The chips can now be cut away (fig. 112) and once removed will appear as shown in fig. 113. Repeat the procedure until the required depth has been obtained (fig. 114), forming the chamfer end. The remainder can now be pared away with a sharp chisel until a plane can once again be brought into use.

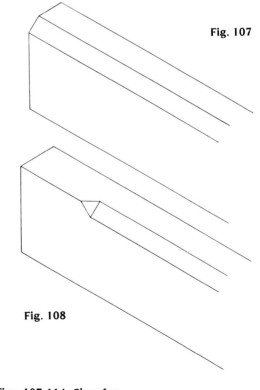

Fig. 107

Fig. 108

Figs. 107-114 Chamfers

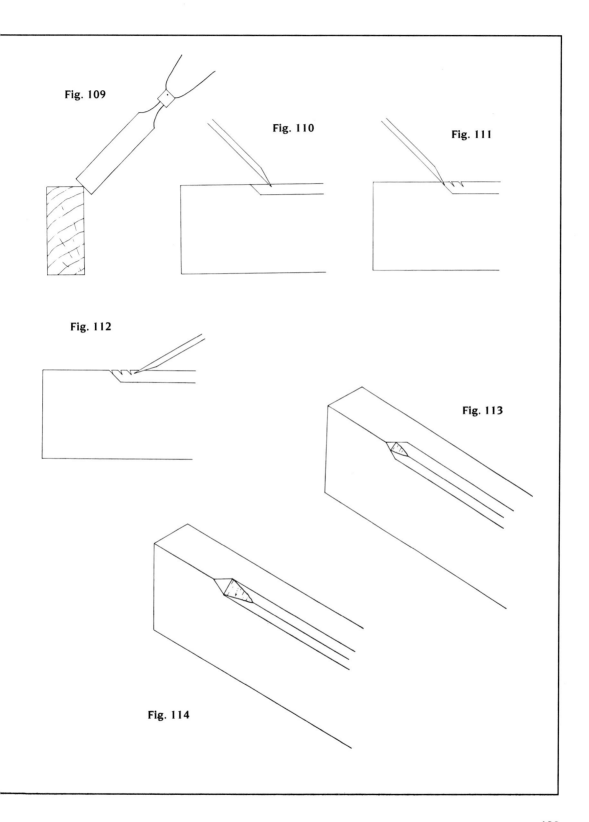

Fig. 109

Fig. 110

Fig. 111

Fig. 112

Fig. 113

Fig. 114

129

Dovetail Joints

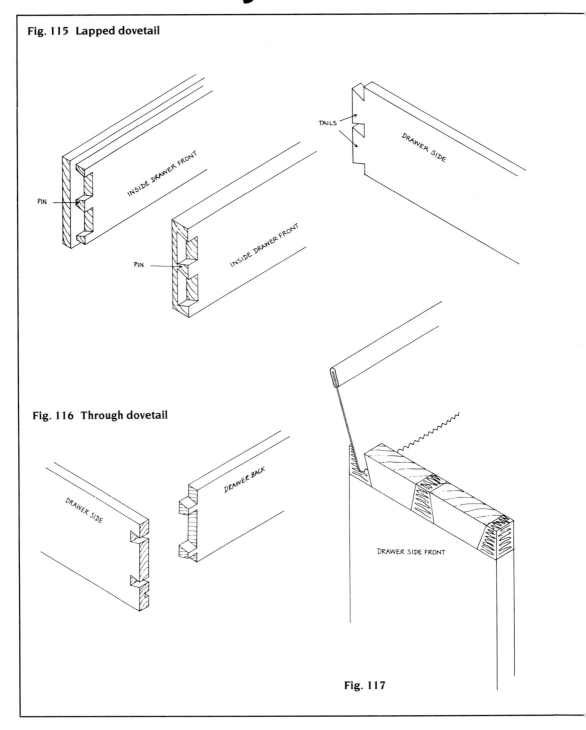

Fig. 115 Lapped dovetail

INSIDE DRAWER FRONT

PIN

PIN

INSIDE DRAWER FRONT

TAILS

DRAWER SIDE

Fig. 116 Through dovetail

DRAWER SIDE

DRAWER BACK

DRAWER SIDE FRONT

Fig. 117

Fig. 118

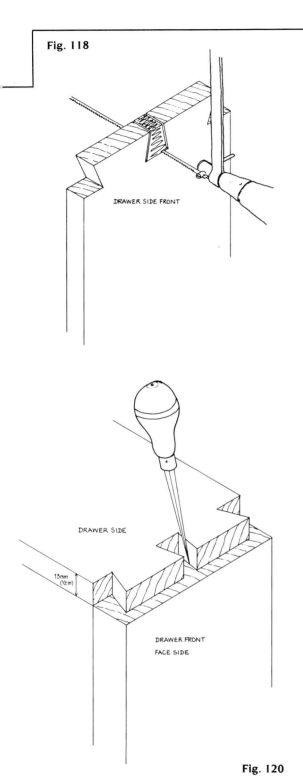

Fig. 119

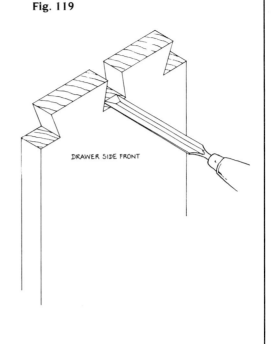

DRAWER SIDE FRONT

DRAWER SIDE FRONT

DRAWER SIDE

13mm
(½in)

DRAWER FRONT
FACE SIDE

Fig. 120

There are two types of dovetail joints used in the construction of drawers in this book. The *lapped dovetail* (fig. 115) is used for fixing the drawer sides to the drawer front, and the *through dovetail* (fig. 116) is used for fixing the sides to the back. Having reached the stage where the dovetails have been marked on the various drawer parts, the first step is cutting them out. Secure the drawer side in a vice and, using a tenon saw, cut down the waste wood side of all front rails to the depth required (fig. 117). Remove the two corner pieces of waste wood using a tenon saw; the centre piece of waste wood (fig. 118), will have to be removed by using a coping saw. Any roughness that the saw has left should be carefully pared away using a sharp chisel (fig. 119). The principle for cutting out the tails on the back of the drawer sides is the same as for the front, and the same procedure should be used. Next, lay the front tails onto the end of the drawer front as shown in fig. 120, and mark their position with a sharp bradawl. The depth of the tail housing will be governed by the thickness of the drawer side tail (in this case 13mm – ½in).

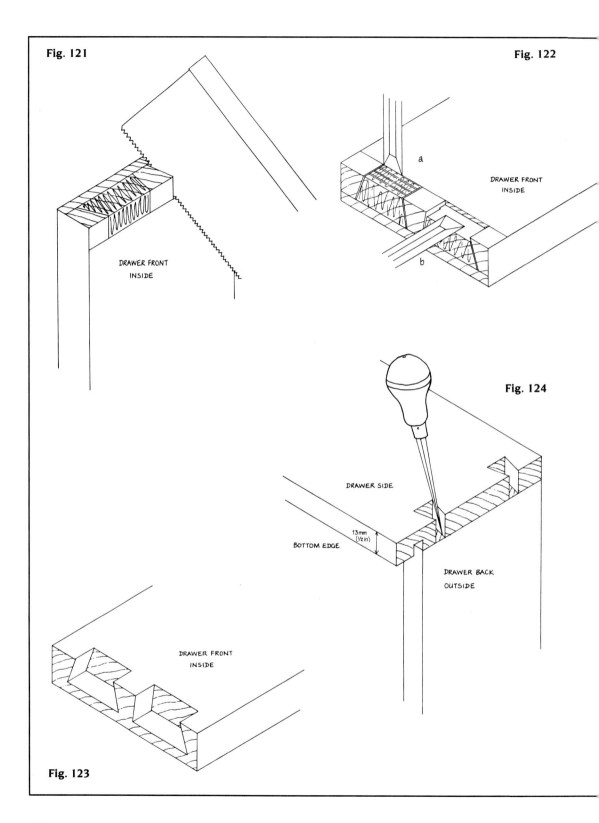

Fig. 121

Fig. 122

DRAWER FRONT
INSIDE

a

b

DRAWER FRONT
INSIDE

Fig. 124

DRAWER SIDE

13mm
(1/2 in)

BOTTOM EDGE

DRAWER BACK
OUTSIDE

DRAWER FRONT
INSIDE

Fig. 123

132

Fig. 125

Fig. 126

Fig. 127

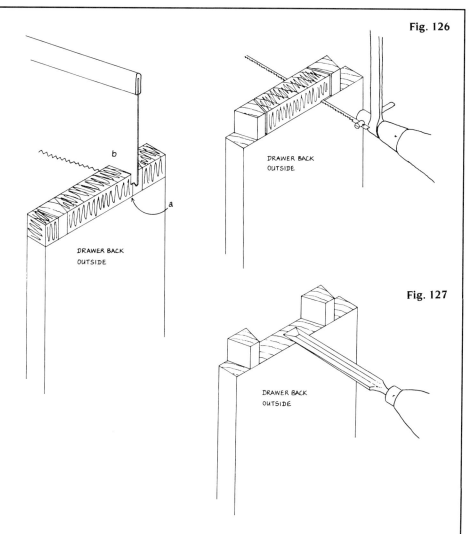

b

a

DRAWER BACK
OUTSIDE

DRAWER BACK
OUTSIDE

DRAWER BACK
OUTSIDE

A tenon saw can now be used to cut down the side of each pin (fig. 121), keeping always on the waste wood side of the line. Then, using a sharp chisel as shown in fig. 122, make a number of cuts down into the tail housing, taking care to keep inside the line. The top 3.2mm (⅛in) or so can now be removed by tapping a chisel into the end (fig. 122). Continue this procedure until all the waste has been removed and the tail housing is as shown in fig. 123.

To cut the pins into the drawer back, lay the drawer side onto the back (fig. 124), and mark their positions with a sharp bradawl. The length of the pin is again governed by the thickness of the drawer side (13mm – ½in), and a pencil or gauge line should be drawn on both sides and ends at this depth (fig. 125). Secure the drawer back in a vice and, using a tenon saw, cut down on the waste wood side of each pin (fig. 125) to the required depth. The corner pieces can now be removed using a tenon saw, but the centre section of waste must be removed with a coping saw (fig. 126). Any roughness that has been left by the saw can be carefully pared away with a sharp chisel (fig. 127). Always try all joints as they are completed to establish a good fit before the final assembly.

⬜⬜ **Mortise and Tenon Joints**

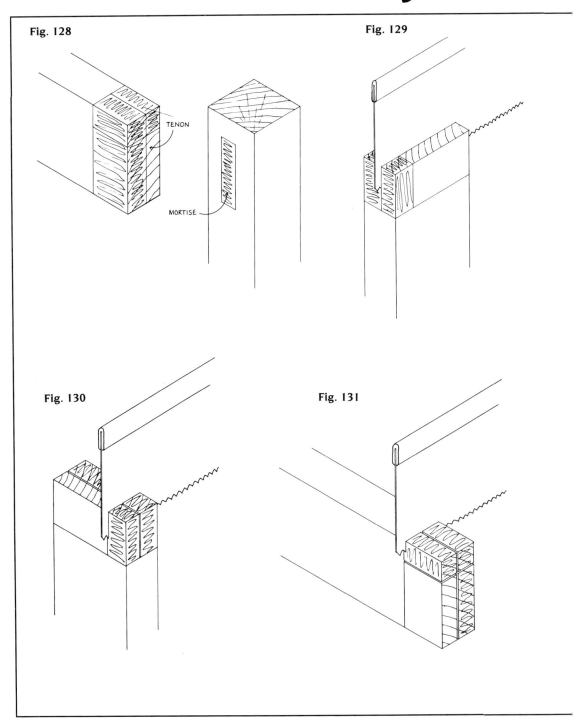

Fig. 128

TENON

MORTISE

Fig. 129

Fig. 130

Fig. 131

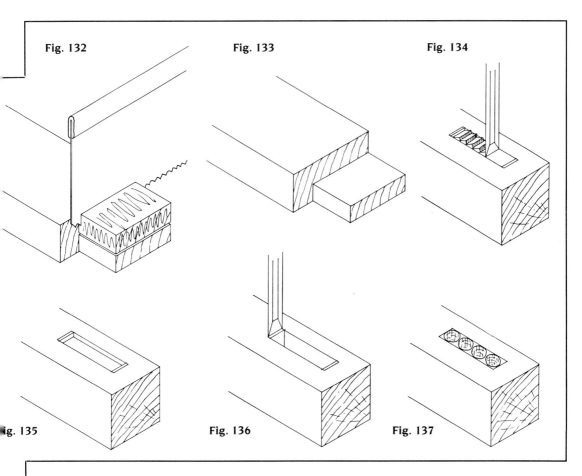

Fig. 132 Fig. 133 Fig. 134

Fig. 135 Fig. 136 Fig. 137

There are many variations of the mortise and tenon joint, though the principles of making it are virtually the same in each case. The joint illustrated has been used many times on rails in this book. Having already prepared the timber by marking the location, size and shape of the joints (fig. 128), the next step is to cut them out. The area that is to be removed on both the mortise and the tenon should be shaded in pencil to avoid the risk of cutting away the wrong piece.

Working first on the tenon, secure the timber firmly in a vice, and with a tenon saw cut down to the pencil line, keeping always on the waste wood side of the line (figs. 129, 130).

Next, clamp the timber lengthways in a vice and cut down to the previous saw cut (fig. 131). The first of the waste wood will now fall away. Lastly, cut the remaining piece of waste wood away (fig. 132). The completed tenon will now appear as illustrated in fig. 133. Any

roughness remaining on the tenon after sawing can be removed using a sharp chisel.

To remove the waste wood from the mortise, select a chisel of the same width as the joint, place it in the centre (fig. 134), and, with a mallet, tap the chisel into the waste, moving the chisel after each blow about 3.2mm ($\frac{1}{8}$in), first towards one end and then the other. When the cuts have all been completed to within 1.5mm ($\frac{1}{16}$in) of each end, the waste chips can be removed as shown in fig. 135. Repeat the process as many times as it takes to reach the desired depth. Lastly, remove the 1.5mm ($\frac{1}{16}$in) of waste wood at either end (fig. 136), so completing the mortise joint.

As an alternative to the above method, drill a number of holes the same width as the mortise to the depth required (fig. 137), and with a chisel of the same width chop out the remaining waste wood until the joint is clean.

⑫ Jointing Boards Edge to Edge

To increase the width of a piece of timber it is necessary to joint two, three or more boards together. This can be done in one of three ways. *Rubbed jointing* involves planing both edges flat, gluing and cramping the boards together – a method best used on boards up to 16mm (⅝in) in thickness. *Dowel jointing* is suitable for boards such as those used on small table tops, and *tongue jointing* is a method used on much heavier work such as jointing boards for the refectory table top. The length of time a glue should be left to dry will depend on the glue used, but 24 hours is usually long enough.

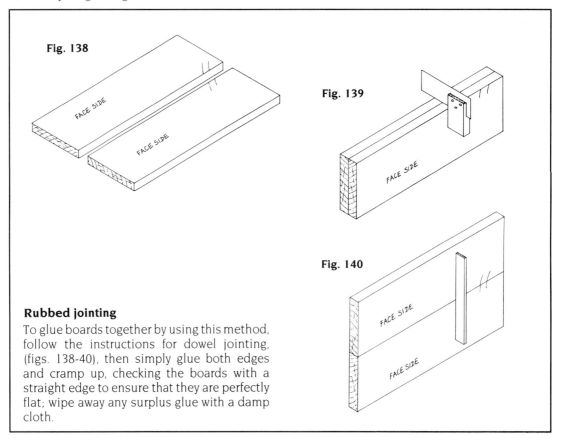

Fig. 138

Fig. 139

Fig. 140

Rubbed jointing

To glue boards together by using this method, follow the instructions for dowel jointing, (figs. 138-40), then simply glue both edges and cramp up, checking the boards with a straight edge to ensure that they are perfectly flat; wipe away any surplus glue with a damp cloth.

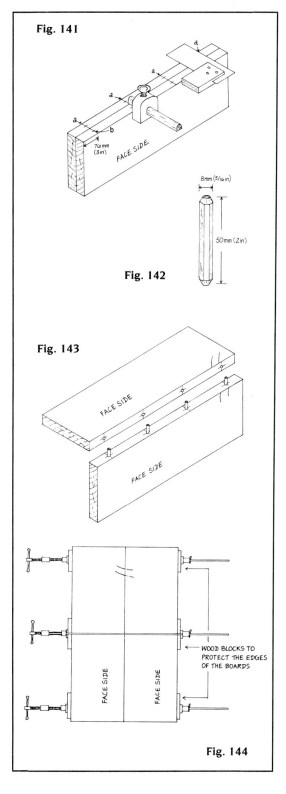

Fig. 141

Fig. 142

Fig. 143

WOOD BLOCKS TO
PROTECT THE EDGES
OF THE BOARDS

FACE SIDE

FACE SIDE

Fig. 144

Dowel jointing

Having chosen the boards, select the sides that are to be the face sides, and the edges that are to be prepared for jointing. Lay them flat, and run two pencil lines across the face sides towards one end (fig. 138). This will show at a glance the position in which the boards are to be jointed during the various stages. Secure the boards in a vice with the face sides out (fig. 139), and plane the edges until they are perfectly square.

Position one board onto the other, checking that the pencil marks correspond and check with a straight edge that the boards are flat (fig. 140). No daylight should show through the joint at any point. When a satisfactory joint has been obtained, place the boards back to back (fig. 141), and secure in a vice or by means of two cramps. At a point about 76mm (3in) from each end, square a line across the edges of the boards (fig. 141). The area between these lines can now be divided up into equal parts, so a line is squared across at intervals of between 152mm (6in) and 229mm (9in). Set a gauge at half the thickness of the board and, working from the face side of each board, mark a line across each pencil line (fig. 141). At the point where the lines cross drill a hole 8mm ($^5/_{16}$in) in diameter, to a depth of 29mm (1$^1/_8$in), in each board. The dowel pegs to be tapped into these holes should have a dull point made at each end (fig. 142), and a sliver of wood removed from the length. This is done to allow the peg to penetrate the hole with ease and trapped air and glue to escape. To joint the boards together, squeeze a blob of glue into each hole and smear a fine layer along both edges. Tap a dowel peg fully home in each of the holes in one board (fig. 143) then position the other board so the holes correspond to the pegs, and push home. The boards can now be cramped as shown in fig. 144, and any surplus glue wiped away with a damp cloth. Leave for about 24 hours to ensure that the glue has properly hardened before working on it further.

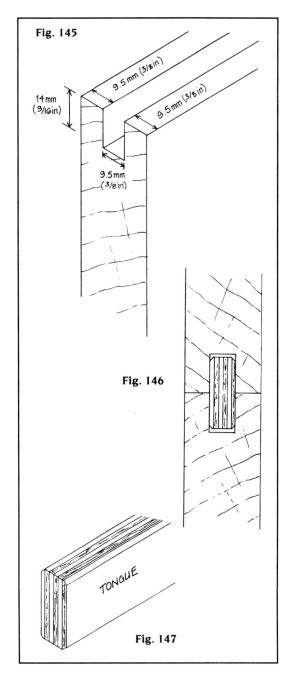

Fig. 145

14mm
(9/16in)

9.5mm (3/8in)

9.5mm (3/8in)

9.5mm
(3/8in)

Fig. 146

TONGUE

Fig. 147

Tongue jointing

When jointing boards by means of a tongue, remember that the width of the groove to house the tongue should ideally be one-third of the thickness of the board, and the depth of the groove should be half the thickness (fig. 145). Prepare the boards to be jointed in the same way as for dowel jointing, up to fig. 140; at this point, working from the face side of each board, a groove should be made the full length of each board, from the dimensions in fig. 145.

The tongue itself is best cut from a piece of cross-grained ply, either as one long length or several short pieces. Cut the tongue about 3.2mm (⅛in) smaller overall than the depth of the two grooves, leaving a gap of about 1.6mm (¹⁄₁₆in) top and bottom (fig. 146), to allow room for glue. Plane the sharp edges from all four corners of the tongue (fig. 147). The tongue should now push into the groove, and without excess pressure being exerted, slide to and fro.

Next, the boards can be jointed. Run glue into each groove and along the edges that are to butt together. Smear a thin film of glue onto the tongue, push the tongue firmly into the groove and butt up the boards together. Cramp up and finish as shown for dowel jointing.

13 Turned Wooden Knobs

Full-size sketches of two turned wooden knobs are shown here. Knob A is suitable for cupboard doors and small drawers and is turned from a piece of timber 38 × 38 × 76mm (1½ × 1½ × 3in). Knob B is a slightly larger knob more suitable for dresser drawers, and is turned from a piece of timber 50 × 50 × 76mm (2 × 2 × 3in).

Fig. 148

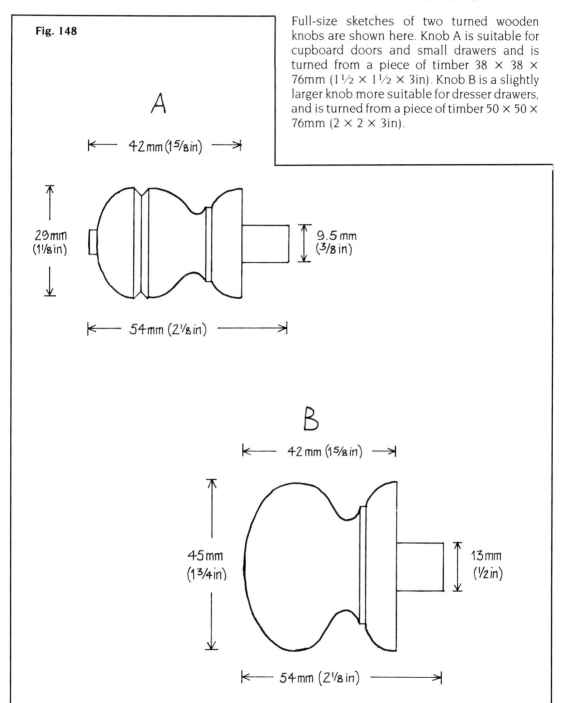

A

42mm (1⁵⁄₈in)

29mm
(1⅛in)

9.5mm
(³⁄₈in)

54mm (2⅛in)

B

42mm (1⁵⁄₈in)

45mm
(1¾in)

13mm
(½in)

54mm (2⅛in)

Suppliers

UK
Wood yards are surprisingly numerous in most parts of the country, and a few minutes spent going through the Yellow Pages will give the location of those in your area. If, however, any difficulty is experienced in obtaining a particular timber, contact:
The Branch Secretary
Timber Trades Federation
47 Whitcombe Street
London WC2H 7DL

USA
For information and advice on obtaining timber in the USA, contact:
The Federal Timber Purchasers Association
3900 South Wadsworth Blvd
201 Denver
Colorado